HISTORICAL NEEDLEWORK

A Study of Influences in Scotland
and Northern England

HISTORICAL NEEDLEWORK

A Study of Influences in Scotland
and Northern England

by

MARGARET H. SWAIN

BARRIE & JENKINS
LONDON

First published 1970 by
Barrie & Jenkins Ltd.,
2 Clement's Inn, London, W.C.2

SBN 257 65213 2

Made and printed in Great Britain by
Cox & Wyman Ltd., London, Fakenham and Reading

Foreword

This is an attempt to take a new look at old needlework in Britain. To describe it century by century, or even reign by reign, may be orderly, but is not always accurate, since taste and design did not change suddenly with the turn of the century, or at each coronation. Indeed, the domestic needlewoman, who made most of the pieces remaining to us in this country, seems to have been very conservative in her choice of designs.

I have taken, instead, well-defined groups of needlework, such as chair seats, bed hangings and pictures, and have selected only pieces that are signed and dated, or otherwise well documented, to serve as reference for those whose dates and history are not known. A great many of the pieces are still in the houses for which they were made, and I am grateful to the owners for allowing me to use them as illustrations. With the exception of white embroidery, which has been my study for many years, I have not dealt with embroidery on clothing, as costume is now an important and separate subject, and in any case, except for underwear, clothing is seldom signed or dated.

Since I have had the good fortune to live in Edinburgh for twenty-two years, I have had unique opportunities of access to public and private archives in Scotland, which have never before been explored for research into historical embroidery, and the new material so obtained sheds a fresh light on the history of needlework over the whole of Britain.

The search for accurate information about the history of embroidery is frequently tantalizing; the facts are often elusive, or have simply not been recorded for an art so homely and universal. The rewards of such a search lie not only in the few facts that one finds in the inventories or accounts that have survived, but also in the friendships made on the way. In this, I have been most fortunate. Experts and scholars, museum curators and librarians, in this country and abroad, have given freely of their knowledge and time, and pointed the way to other directions for my search. I owe my gratitude to many, but must mention especially the late Mrs. Nancy Groves Cabot, who shared with me her wide knowledge of the engraved sources of needlework designs, and gave me most affectionate encouragement; Mr. John L. Nevinson whose wide erudition and advice has been always promptly and generously available; Lady Victoria Wemyss who showed me the wealth of historical needlework still surviving in private houses in Britain. In addition, I must thank Mr. Revel Oddy, of the Royal Scottish Museum, and Mr. Stuart Maxwell of the National Museum of Scottish Antiquities, who have over the years encouraged me with help and advice.

I am deeply grateful to all the owners for allowing their embroideries to be illustrated in this book, most of them for the first time, and to the photographers whose skill has shown the embroideries so clearly; especially must I thank Mr. T. C. Dodds, F.I.M.L.T., F.I.I.P., F.R.P.S., and Mr. Ronald Stewart, who photographed many of the pieces specially for me. My thanks are also due to the Chairman and Secretary of the National Art-Collections Fund for allowing me to use some of the blocks from the catalogue of the exhibition *Needlework from Scottish Country Houses,* and to Thames and Hudson Ltd. for assistance in obtaining a print for Plate I which also appears in their publication *The Royal Hordes* by E. D. Phillips.

The book would not have been written at all without the constant support and encouragement of my husband.

No bibliography is included, as full references are given after each chapter.

MARGARET H. SWAIN
Edinburgh, 1969.

Contents

List of Plates

Those printed in bold type are in colour

15. Detail of crewel work from large hanging on cotton/linen twill stamped "1640 Bruges". *The Earl of Elgin and Kincardine.*

16. Detail showing the Hamilton crest, dated 1699, from a set of bed hangings. *Lady Broun Lindsay.*

17. Portion of a bed valance. Coloured silks on linen. *The Earl of Haddington.*

18. Detail of bed curtain, Wemyss Castle. Also an enlarged detail, showing initials and the date 1729, and a diagram giving the names.

19. Needlework picture. "Abraham entertaining the angels." *Royal Scottish Museum.*

20. Engraving by Gerard de Jode. Antwerp, 1585. "Abraham entertaining the angels." *National Library of Scotland.*

21. The Mellerstain Panel, 1706. *The Earl of Haddington.*

22. Engraving. "Smelling", from "The Five Senses". *The Earl of Haddington.*

23. Page from the *Book of Beast . . .*, published by Thomas Johnson, London, 1630. *The Earl of Haddington.*

24. Large panel from St. Nicholas Kirk, Aberdeen. "Esther before Ahasuerus." *The Kirk Session of St. Nicholas Kirk, Aberdeen.*

25. Engraving. "Esther before Ahasuerus", after M. van Heemskercke, published by N. Visscher, c. 1660. *British Museum.*

26. Two panels of a six fold screen signed and dated "Julia Calverly 1727". Wallington Hall, Northumberland. *The National Trust.*

27. Engraving. "The Swarming of Bees", book IV of Virgil's *Georgics*, by W. Hollar from the design by Francis Cleyn. *The University Library, Edinburgh.*

28. Engraving. "The Making of Agricultural Implements", by W. Hollar from the design by Francis Cleyn. *The University Library, Edinburgh.*

29. Wall hanging, signed and dated, "Anne Grant 1750". *Lady Jean Grant of Monymusk.*

30. Wall panel from a set designed by Robert Adam. *Major R. T. Hog of Newliston.*

31. Felt flower picture, 1790. *Lady Victoria Wemyss.*

32. Detail from a panel, a mounted horseman with the initials KI for King James 1. *Jedburgh Town Council.*

33. St. Wenceslas. Figure in high relief on a chasuble dated 1487. Moravian. *Moravska Galerie, Brno, Czechoslovakia.*

34. Mantle of the Order of the Thistle, 1687.

35. Casket by Hannah Smith, 1654–1656. *The Whitworth Art Gallery, Manchester.*

36. Lid of casket by Hannah Smith. "Joseph being raised from the Pit." *The Whitworth Art Gallery, Manchester.*

37. Engraving. "Joseph being raised from the Pit", by Gerard de Jode. Antwerp, 1585. *National Library of Scotland.*

38. Part of a linen sampler signed by Mary Lawley, 1667, with padded figure wearing detached lace stitch garments. *Mr. Gervase Riddell-Carre.*

39. The Mary Erskine table carpet. Turkey work. *The Master's Court of the Company of Merchants of the City of Edinburgh.*

40. Unused chair seat from a set of twelve. *The Earl of Wemyss and March.*

41. Unused chair back, now a cushion cover, from a set of nine backs and two seats. *The Earl of Wemyss and March.*

42. Gilt chair, covers of Gobelins tapestry, made for the Tapestry Room at Croome Court, Worcestershire, c. 1769. *Metropolitan Museum, New York.*

43. Mahogany chair with fish scale carving, 1756. *The Duke of Atholl.*

44. Gilt chair made by Chipchase and Lambert, 1783. *The Duke of Atholl.*

45. Chair from a set of ten with settee. *Sir Mark Dalrymple, Bt.*

46. Engraving. "Paysanne de Brabant", by Bernard Picart, Amsterdam, 1728. *Foundation Atlas van Stolk, Rotterdam.*

47. Sampler, one of a pair now mounted in a Chippendale firescreen, showing designs and stitches for chair seats. *Edinburgh Corporation, Lauriston Castle.*

48. Sampler of Betty Plenderleath, 1745. *Royal Scottish Museum.*

49. Sampler of Elizabeth Gardner, 1818. *The Misses Muirhead.*

50. Sampler of Elizabeth Gardner, 1820. *The Misses Muirhead.*

51. Sampler of Elizabeth Gardner, 1821. *The Misses Muirhead.*

52. White sampler signed C M S 1678, Swedish. *Nordiska Museet.*

53. Sampler of Elizabeth Gardner, 1822. *The Misses Muirhead.*

54. Sampler of lace fillings signed MARY QUELCH 1609. *Dr. Douglas Goodhart.*

55. Sampler signed "Jenny Grant 1724–1725". *National Museum of Scottish Antiquities.*

56. Shirt ruffle in Dresden work, said to have been worn by Prince Charles Edward Stuart in 1745. *Royal Scottish Museum.*

57. Kerchief, signed and dated R. L. 1752, for Rachel Leonard of Norton, Massachusetts. *Museum of Fine Arts, Boston.*

58. Apron said to have been worn at the christening of Prince Charles Edward Stuart, 1721. *The Burrell Collection, Glasgow.*

59. Flounce, detail showing tambour stitch and Dresden work.

60. Lower hem and flounce of a baby robe in Ayrshire embroidery.

61. Bodice of baby robe and detail of skirt. *Mrs. Arthur.*

62. Cap crown.

63. Baby cap in Ayrshire embroidery.

64. Berlin woolwork picture inscribed "The Young Bruce, First Lord of Canada", 1849–1854. *The Earl of Elgin and Kincardine.*

65. Unused carpet square in Berlin woolwork with green ground, 1853. *Lady Broun Lindsay*

66. Panel from a four-leaved screen composed of twelve panels of Berlin woolwork, 1860. *Esdaile School, Edinburgh.*

67. Slipper tops in Berlin woolwork inscribed "To Mr. E. Mcrae from an admirer".

68. White work panel worked by Lady Evelyn Stuart Murray. *The Duke of Atholl.*

A Study of Influences

If we are to believe the Bible, needlework was first practised in the Garden of Eden, where Adam and Eve, knowing themselves to be naked, sewed fig leaves together to make themselves aprons. Like gardening, whose roots are also in Paradise, needlework is so universal that it is accepted as a basic human accomplishment. Gardening can be wholly utilitarian, producing fruit and vegetables for our sustenance, or it can rise to the level of a minor art, "without which" (said Bacon) "buildings and palaces are but gross handyworks". Needlework, too, can be utilitarian, providing the bare necessities of cover and warmth for our nakedness, but it can also flower into a symbolic art as it did in the medieval church, where embroidery took its part with music, sculpture and painting to provide a worthy setting for the liturgy.

We do not know the flowers that bloomed in the Hanging Gardens of Babylon, nor even the smell of a rose in Shakespeare's time. Pictures and descriptions are all that remain of medieval gardens. But the needlework of past centuries still survives, fragile but enduring, each patient stitch visible, a small relic of the industry and taste of the time, more evocative and personal than stone carving or metalwork. We can still see, in Durham Cathedral, the exquisite stole and maniple of St. Cuthbert, embroidered around 909–916 A.D., probably at Winchester. It was never worn by St. Cuthbert, who died on Farne Island in 687, but was found in his coffin, probably placed there in the reign of King Athelstan 924–940. But it is not as a relic of the saint that we value it most. These narrow strips of embroidery are the only surviving examples in Britain of ecclesiastical textiles of the late Saxon church. The finely laid gold threads, held down by silk, portray the tiny figures of grave saints, draped in liturgical robes and flanked by decorative lettering. The assured meticulous technique is evidence of the superlative craftsmanship of the period, and the design shows that the products of Byzantine silk and embroidery workshops had already reached these islands.

Embroidery should not be dismissed as the elegant pastime of ladies with leisured hours to fill. It was never an exclusively female occupation, even in Britain. In the Orient there are male embroiderers to this day. Needles and thread have been used since the dawn of history as a means of textile decoration, and needlework provides rich source material for the social and economic historian, offering evidence of the taste and background of those who made it.

Archaeologists are well aware of the value of the textiles they excavate; even fragments of a simple weave of woollen or linen cloth can yield useful information. But how evocative and revealing is the embroidered face of that nomad warrior, with his moustache and alert gaze worked in wool on repp, now in the Hermitage museum, Leningrad (Plate 1). It was excavated at Noin-Ula, Northern Mongolia, and was made in the first century before Christ. An even earlier piece of embroidery was found with others at Patzyryk in 1950. Probably worked in the fifth century before Christ, it has a brilliantly vital running phoenix, worked in the familiar chain stitch in silk. It reveals how sophisticated Chinese silk dyeing and embroidery was even at that early date.

Textiles are rightly regarded as precious evidence of the trade and civilization of the people who lived in the cities that are excavated by archaeologists. Textiles which are embroidered have an additional artistic value, even if they lack the startling impact of the nomad's gaze from Noin-Ula. Climate, trade and religion, as well as taste, influenced the needlework made in a country at a certain time. It is no accident that the German medieval embroidery, *Opus Teutonicum* should be worked on linen with linen thread. Regensburg on the Danube, and Constance, where the Rhine flows out of the Lake, were the two great centres for the flax-producing countries of central Europe and Italy, and both were medieval markets for linen. Convents on the waterways controlled by these two cities were well placed to obtain the durable evenly woven linen, and to work it in its own thread in a dazzling variety of geometrical stitches, counted by the thread.

The history of embroidery is often narrowly taught and is frequently described in an insular fashion in this country, as if needlework had hardly existed outside Britain. Yet museums have large collections of foreign embroideries which were brought here by travellers and businessmen, as presents for their wives and families and treasured as exotic curiosities. In the galleries they are separated into countries and into centuries; and so, they remain separated in our minds, as if anything as portable as a textile could not be copied outside its own frontier, using perhaps similar thread on an indigenous material. Although it is tempting and orderly to classify needlework into centuries, it is completely misleading. Design did not change suddenly at the beginning of each century. It did not, indeed, change so rapidly as we are apt to imagine, for it was often copied from a picture or a book made fifty years earlier.

As a trading nation Britain was peculiarly open to the influence of new fashions and techniques from the Continent and the Far East. Fine linen came from the Low Countries, muslin from India, canvas from France and silks from the Levant. It is these varied importations of materials and designs that has made British embroidery so diverse and unorthodox.

Almost no style is indigenous, though all are transmuted into a native and recognizable type mainly because since the Reformation embroidery in Britain had become domestic, not professional. It has an uninhibited individuality, which is missing from the immaculate technique of the workshops of France and Italy, which had to compete for the custom of wealthy patrons.

Those who could afford it, of course, imported their own tapestries and textiles; those who could not, for a variety of reasons and needs, made their own. Climate must have made bed curtains a sheer necessity in the unheated houses of Scotland and the north of England, where they remained in fashion long after they had been discarded in the south. Wall hangings gave warmth and colour in the long dark months of winter. This tendency is well illustrated in the Scottish family of Campbell of Glenorchy, who became rich and powerful during the sixteenth century in Breadalbane around Loch Tay, mainly because the clan controlled one of the two main routes to the north. All the ladies appear to have been excellent needlewomen, and at first produced their own hangings, helped, no doubt, by members of their household. Katherine Ruthven, second wife of Sir Colin Campbell of Glenorchy, (they were married in 1550), made bed valances embroidered with her arms and initials. One set has survived, and is now in the Burrell Collection, Glasgow. (Plate 10). She made cushions and coverings as well. Her son's wife was also a needlewoman, and the Campbell inventory for the year 1598 lists 98 serviettes "maid be the Ladie of new lynnings" (that is, hemmed by her) as well as "3 do. markit with blew silk".[1]

But as the family got wealthier, they no longer depended on homespun linen, hemmed at home. In 1632 the next Laird paid 700 merks for "damas naprie out of West Flanders", and "silk beddis and other furniture", as well as paying 1,500 merks for "fine Arras hingings for decorment of his home". This did not prevent his wife from making yet another valance to add to the family collection. She put her initials on it, together with her husband's and the Campbell arms.[2] She had no children, so because she had made it herself, she took it with her back to her brother's house, Loudon Castle in Ayrshire (as she was entitled to do) when her husband died in 1640.

Climate, trade, politics and religion have all influenced the existence of needlework in the past, not only determining what was embroidered, but also what was destroyed. The accident that caused England to adopt the Lutheran reformed religion, while Scotland followed the teachings of Calvin, resulted in the salvaging of some of the needlework of the medieval church in England, whereas nothing was spared in Scotland. A century after the Reformation in Scotland, a mob arrived at the Roman Catholic house of Traquair in 1688 to celebrate the Glorious Revolution, the arrival of the Protestant William and Mary after the flight of James VII and II. They seized "5 vestments, belonging to a priest . . . one of silk curiously embroidered with gold and silver

4

A STUDY OF INFLUENCES

thread . . . Mary and the Babe in a caise, most curiously wrought with a kind of pearl; Agnus Dei of lamber (amber) . . . an large broad (sic) opening with two leaves, covered within with cloth of gold, having a vail covering the middle part, wherein were sued severall superstitious pictures . . . (relics and) an embroidered eucharist box, (two) embroidered crucifixes . . ."

"Having heard they had conveyed severall trinkets to another place, they went and searched the same and found therin a massy Eucharist silver cup (two) silver candlesticks, (two) silver eucharist tranchers . . . a cloath of silk four-cornered richly embroidered with silver, having the shape of a dove in the middle . . .

All solemnly burnt at the Cross at Peebles."[3]

REFERENCES

1. INNES, C. [ed.], *The Black Book of Taymouth*, Bannatyne Club, 1855, p. 327.

2. Now in the Metropolitan Museum, New York. See STANDEN, E., "Two Scottish Embroideries in the Metropolitan Museum", *Connoisseur*, Vol. CXXXIX, 1957, pp. 196–200.

3. University Library, Edinburgh. Laing Coll. MS. Vol. 1. p. 460 1.336.

Before the Reformation

In England, many of the pieces that escaped destruction during the Reformation are of *Opus Anglicanum*,[1] the English church embroidery which was so prized by Continental churchmen in the thirteenth and fourteenth centuries. It was flat and flexible, which made it eminently suitable for vestments. This was due to the underside couching employed for the gold and silver thread, whereby the metal, instead of lying flat on the surface, was pulled through the linen foundation, making an angle at each stitch. At its best, *Opus Anglicanum* had a refined delicacy because of its superlative technique and because split stitch in silk modelled the draperies, and in circular whorls, shaped the cheekbones of the saints and angels depicted on its surface. It owes some of its excellence to the fact that it coincided with so rich a period of religious illustration in the south of England, as may be seen in contemporary illuminated manuscripts. The elegant linear figures in manuscripts illuminated, for instance, by Matthew Paris of St Albans (1217–1257), with their delicately tinted outlines, are closely related to those on chasubles and copes, some of them now sadly mutilated, which have survived the wear of centuries and the destruction of the Reformers.

Opus Anglicanum was highly professional, designed and made in workshops in London and perhaps in East Anglia, by male as well as female embroiderers. The designs were made to order, showing the arms and chosen saints of those who ordered them. The workshops in London were geographically conveniently situated to export their vestments to the Continent. After the Black Death, 1348–9, the epidemic of bubonic plague which had spread to England from the Continent, the number of workmen was decimated in this as in other trades, and as a result in order to economize in labour as well as materials, a new technique was developed. Individual figures and motifs were worked in silk and gold, before being applied to a cope or altar hanging of velvet or damask, whose woven design took the place of the tedious finely-couched gold background of the earlier work. This was quicker and cheaper, and some might claim more practical, since the richly embroidered motifs could be re-applied to new material, if the velvet or damask wore out. This type of applied embroidery was not, of course, confined to Britain, but was widely used in all European countries.

No doubt other ecclesiastical centres in Britain, the cathedrals and abbeys, employed embroiderers to make and repair their vestments and the altar hangings and linen required in liturgical use. Probably also, in medieval as in later centuries, some nuns in convents undertook the repair and making of vestments and altar linen.

In Scotland, little church needlework escaped the Reformation except the so-called Fetternear Banner[2] and a corporal and chalice veil,[3] and these have only survived by a curious chance: the Fetternear Banner because it was put away unfinished, the other two because they were made into covers for documents in the eighteenth century, at which time they were laid in a drawer. Inventories show that Scotland had church needlework in quantities comparable with other Christian countries, but only fragments of medieval gold work survive.

Iconoclasm was more thorough in Scotland during the Reformation than in any other European country. Even Edinburgh's flag did not escape the zeal of the reformers. On June 24th 1562, the provost, baillies and Council "ordanis the idole Sanct Geyell (Giles) to be cuttit forth of the townys standart and the thrissill (thistle) put in place thairof, and that the thesaurer furnis taffete to the samyn". The destruction of church needlework was not entirely due to Calvinist iconoclasm, however, but was partly the result of shortage of cash and a native thrift. In 1561, vestments and plate from the Kirk of St. Giles, Edinburgh, which had been distributed to members of the Burgh Council for safe-keeping, were sold, probably for the gold and jewels on them, in order to pay the stipend of John Knox, the Calvinist Reformer :

April 5th. The Baillies and counsall ordains the vestmentis and kirk gear to be gadderit and sauld with diligence, and of the reddiest money thairof the fyfty pund debursit and deliverit be Maister James Watsoun (Dean of Guild) to Johne Knox be refundit and payit to him agane.

On May 27th the Council ordained that:

The Kaipis (Copes) Vestmentis and alter grayth (furnishings) quilk pertaineth to Sanct Gelys alter presentlie in handis or so far as may be gotten in, to be deliverit to David Somer, baillie, and to James Barroun, and they to dispone the samyn to the maist advantage. . . . The Baillies and haill counsall ordainis James Watsoun, dene of gyld, incontinent to deliver to Johne Knox, minister, the sowme of fyfte pundis for his quarter payment.[4]

It was not only the Calvinist baillies, however, who put church vestments to a profane use. In 1562 the rebel Earl of Huntly was defeated by the Queen's troops and he died suddenly after the battle of Corrichie, Aberdeenshire. His body was transported to Edinburgh, where it was roughly embalmed by an Edinburgh physician, and then tried for treason in the presence of Mary Queen of Scots. His belongings were sent by sea from Aberdeen to Leith, and carefully listed by the Queen's valet de chambre, Servais de Conde. They included ten copes, chasubles and tunicles, "all of claith of gold and thre of thame figurit with reid, and the rest with quhite and yallow", which are thought to have been entrusted to the Catholic Earl of Huntly by the provost and clergy of Aberdeen Cathedral. A note appended to the inventory shows that from them a cope, chasuble and four tunicles were all "brokin and cuttit in hir awin presence" to make a bed for Darnley, while in March 1567 "I deliverit thre of the fairest quilk the Quene gaif to the Lord Bothwell".[5]

In March 1565 three copes, two tunicles and a chasuble of green

8

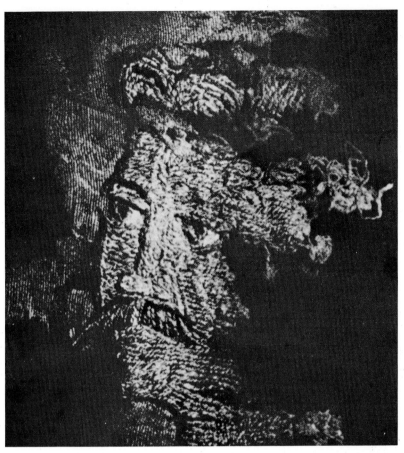

Plate 1. Fragment. Head of a Hun from Noin-Ula, Northern Mongolia.
Wools on woollen repp. c. 1st century B.C. 29 x 14cm.
The Hermitage, Leningrad

Plate 2. The Fetternear Banner.
The centre panel shows the Christ of Pity surrounded by the Instruments of
the Passion. Top left are the arms of Gavin Douglas, Bishop of Dunkeld
(1515–22) and Provost of St. Giles, Edinburgh from 1503 to about 1522. He
was exiled in 1521 and died in 1522 which may account for the incomplete
unused state of the banner.
Coloured silks on fine linen.
Double running stitch (reversible). 1518–22.   149·9 × 79·06 cm.
The National Museum of Antiquities of Scotland, Edinburgh

Plate 3. Woodcut c. 1500, Netherlandish. The Man of Sorrows standing, with the Instruments of Passion.
Sch.893. C.D.1.65. A36(1·) 10.8 x 7.6cm.
The British Museum

Plate 4. Detail of the Fetternear Banner, showing double running stitch (Holbein stitch) used as a filling stitch, alike on both sides.

The National Museum of Antiquities of Scotland, Edinburgh

Plate 5. Portrait of Agnes Keith, wife of the Regent Moray (half brother of Mary Queen of Scots), showing cuffs and small upstanding ruff decorated with blackwork in double running or Holbein stitch, the same stitch as that used on the Fetternear Banner. c. 1561. H. Eworth.

The Earl of Moray

Plate 6(a). Hanging believed to have come from the Palace of Linlithgow.
Heraldic lions with plants.
Black velvet appliqué and yellow silk embroidery on red woollen material.
Laid, satin and couched stitches. 147.5 x 100cm. no.1931 54.
The Royal Scottish Museum, Edinburgh

Plate 6(b). Detail of hanging believed to have come from the Palace of Linlithgow. no.1931 54.
The Royal Scottish Museum, Edinburgh

Plate 7. Valance (detail) Griffin and strawberry plant. The valance shows the arms and initials of Sir Colin Campbell of Glenorchy and his wife, Julian Campbell of Loudon.

Plate 7. Cross stitch in wool on linen. 1631-40. Valance measures 40.6 x 309.8cm. no.54711.

The Metropolitan Museum of Art, New York (Gift of Irwin Untermyer 1954)

Plate 8. Panel. Unused and uncut designs. Animals at the base of trees, with birds and beasts around two sides. The griffin (top centre) repeated at the foot, is the mirror image of the griffin in Plate 7..
Coloured wool and silk on canvas.
Fine tent stitch. 85 x 66.9cm.
Mr. Peter Maxwell Stuart of Traquair

velvet, probably also from Aberdeen Cathedral, were "employit be the Quenis command" and used to cover various articles of furniture. The embroidery was removed to decorate a bed, the green velvet was used for a high chair, two stools, and a *chaise percée*.[6] Vestments of cloth of gold were cut up and given to the Queen's embroiderers to be applied to beds, cloths of estate over the royal chairs, hangings and clothing. This practice was not, however, confined to Scotland. A few years later, the Countess of Shrewsbury (Bess of Hardwick) the Queen's custodian for seventeen years of her long imprisonment in England, used "copes of tissue, cloth of gold" in needlework at Chatsworth.[7] Two of the large hangings, now at Hardwick, depicting Penelope and Lucretia, show appliqué of cloth of gold, as do the screen panels in the High Great Chamber of the same house. They may have come from monastic houses, like the monastic stonework which was carted away to build new houses, just as the monks themselves at St. Albans, had used the Roman tiles of nearby Verulamium to build their abbey church.

It is therefore all the more remarkable that the Fetternear Banner should have survived. It may accurately be described as incomparable, for nothing either in Britain, or so far, in Continental museums has been found with which to compare it. Mgr. David McRoberts has described the banner in detail and has given cogent reasons for dating it between the years 1518 and 1522.[8] It consists of a panel of fine linen, worked in coloured silks, showing in the centre, the blood-flecked figure of Christ as the Image of Pity, pointing to His pierced side, and surrounded by the Instruments of the Passion, including the head of Judas with a money bag, and the head of the Jew who spat upon Christ. (Plate 2.) The top of the panel is unfinished. Surrounding it are three borders: one showing the beads of the Rosary, another an interlace design suggesting the knotted cordeliere of a religious confraternity, and the outermost unfinished, but decorated with scallop shells and columbine flowers. Two completed coats of arms show it to have been made for the Confraternity of the Holy Blood at St. Giles, Edinburgh, during the provostship of Gavin Douglas, Bishop of Dunkeld, who was exiled in 1521 and died in 1522. It was probably his disgrace and death which caused the embroidery, on which his arms were already worked, to be put away unfinished. Its remarkable condition is due to the fact that it has been rarely used, even after it was presented to the Catholic church of Our Lady of the Garioch and St. John in the district of Fetternear in 1859. It is now in the National Museum of Scottish Antiquities, Edinburgh.

Medieval devotion to the Holy Blood of Christ was particularly centred in the city of Bruges, where the famous relic of the Holy Blood was preserved, and where Scottish merchants traded, particularly in cloth and linen; indeed, the fine linen of the banner is almost certainly Flemish. The design, the suffering figure of Christ, and the Instruments of the Passion, is comparatively rare in Britain, though it is to be seen in Netherlandish woodcuts of the period (Plate 3) and was popular in the Netherlands and southern Germany from the fourteenth to the eighteenth centuries. The rococo pilgrimage church of Wies, in Bavaria, was built by Zimmerman in 1746–1754 to house just such a blood-flecked figure of Christ, carved in wood.

There is, however, no reason to doubt that the Fetternear Banner was embroidered in Edinburgh. Its unfinished state and close connexion with the High Kirk of St. Giles make the assumption irresistible. It is not an amateur piece and Mgr. McRoberts names several professional embroiderers working in Edinburgh at the time. Its technique is assured and appears to be unique. It is completely double-sided except for the lettering I N R I which cannot be reversed on the T-shaped cross. The stitch is double-running (Holbein stitch) used as outline and also as a filling (Plate 4), it is worked with such discipline and rhythm that twilled or chevron patterns emerge for instance, on the coats of arms. No other instance of the stitch being used in this way as a filling in Britain has been found, though it appears to be the same stitch as that found in Middle Eastern embroideries of the eighteenth century. It is an admirably economical way of working double-sided embroidery, especially if the piece were indeed intended to be seen from both sides as in the case of a banner. The material and silks seem rather fragile for this purpose, and it has been suggested that it might have been intended as one of a pair of side curtains, attached to the altar by rods. But no reference has been found to decorated side curtains, nor has any picture been found. They are invariably depicted made of plain material.

Double-running, or Holbein stitch worked in black silk geometrically, according to the thread of the material, usually on white linen, is, of course, to be found on the *blackwork* of the period, usually decorating clothing, collars, cuffs, sleeves and caps. Blackwork, if it was used in Scotland, has not survived except in portraits, such as that of Agnes Keith and her husband, the Regent Moray, painted by Hans Eworth, 1561. (Plate 5.) This may have been an imported fashion from England, for in Edinburgh Castle in 1578, amongst garments left by Mary Queen of Scots are "foure Inglis sarkes (chemises) with blak werk" and "ane Inglis sark of quheit werk".

Although the same reversible stitch (double-running or Holbein) is used both in blackwork and in the Fetternear Banner, the effect is entirely different. In blackwork, the spaces are filled with delicately etched geometrical lines. In the Fetternear Banner the stitch is used with great virtuosity to give a richly woven silk pattern on the surface of the fine linen, modelling in sharp detail the gaunt features of Christ, the Instruments of the Passion, the heraldic shields and the tracery of the borders. Like St. Cuthbert's stole at Durham, which is a symbol of the richness of embroidery in the Saxon church, the Fetternear Banner remains a tantalizing and enigmatic relic of the wealth of ecclesiastical textiles, destroyed at the Reformation.

REFERENCES

1. See CHRISTIE, MRS. A. G. I., *English Medieval Embroidery*, Oxford, 1938; and KING, D., *Opus Anglicanum*, Victoria and Albert Museum, 1963.

2. MCROBERTS, D., "The Fetternear Banner," *Innes Review*, Edinburgh, Vol. VII, 1956, p. 69.

3. MCROBERTS, D., "Scottish Medieval Chalice Veils," *Innes Review*, Edinburgh, Vol. XV, 1964, p. 103.

4. Extracts from the *Records of the Burgh of Edinburgh*, 1561.

5. *Inventaires de la Royne Descosse*, 1556–1569, Bannatyne Club, Edinburgh, 1863, p. 53.

6. Op. Cit., p. 153.

7. WINGFIELD DIGBY, G., *Elizabethan Embroidery*, Faber and Faber, London, 1963, p. 62.

8. MCROBERTS, D., "The Fetternear Banner," *Innes Review*, Edinburgh, Vol. VII.

3

Mary Queen of Scots

Even today, three centuries after her death, Mary Queen of Scots excites curiosity and violent partizanship. The dramatic events of her life, followed by her long captivity and execution, together with her undoubted love of needlework, have given rise to a multitude of romantic legends. In the past, so much has been attributed to her needle, while she was in Scotland, that she could scarcely have had time to do anything else but embroider. Now, only two or three pieces, worked during her captivity in England, are conceded to her.

She was born on December 8th, 1542 at Linlithgow Palace, the third and only surviving child of James V and his wife, Mary of Lorraine. Six days after she was born, her father died, suddenly and mysteriously, and she succeeded to the throne of Scotland. When she was nearly six, she was sent to France to be brought up with the children of Henry II and Catherine de Medici, learning needlework among her other accomplishment at the brilliant French court. Her mother remained in Scotland, acting as Regent for part of her daughter's childhood.

In 1558 Mary was married to the Dauphin, Francis, eldest son of Henry II. The following year Henry died and Mary and her husband became King and Queen of France. This was the most brilliant point in her career. The following year, 1560, was disastrous. In June, her mother, the Queen Regent, died in Edinburgh. In August, the Scottish parliament adopted the Calvinist faith for Scotland, and in December, seventeen months after she had become Queen of France, her husband died, and Mary became a widow just before her eighteenth birthday.

She returned to govern Scotland in August 1561, and less than six tempestuous years were to elapse before she was imprisoned by her nobles on the island of Lochleven. During these six years she was so actively involved in government that it is highly improbable that she could have undertaken any of the large pieces of needlework, such as bed hangings or valances, that have been attributed to her during her brief reign in Scotland. That she did some needlework is without question, for the English envoy, Randolph, wrote to his mistress, Queen Elizabeth on October 24th, 1561, soon after Mary's return to Scotland: "I was sent for into the Council Chamber, where she herself ordinarily sitteth the most part of the time, sowing some work or other."[1] But a piece which required a large frame, such as a valance, would have been quite unsuited to her way of life as she journeyed round her kingdom.[2]

She led an energetic life during these years. She hunted, rode to the north, visited her castles at Stirling, Linlithgow, Falkland and Lochleven; she married Darnley, and rode with him at the head of her troops on the *Chaseabout Raid*, when her rebellious lords fled over the border into England. She bore a son, the future James I of Great Britain. Darnley was murdered, and she married Bothwell within three months. A month later, she was imprisoned by her nobles on Lochleven, where she remained for ten months, only to escape into a longer captivity in England.

Yet even if the output of her needle was less than has been believed, her taste and influence, and the influence of the French court where she spent her youth, is incalculable, not only in Scotland, but in England on that other notable needlewoman, the Countess of Shrewsbury ("Bess of Hardwick"), in whose custody she remained for fifteen years of her captivity.

The Kings of Scotland had long employed male (and female) embroiderers for heraldic work and costume embroidery. In 1449 John Sprunt "le broudare" is named. In 1531 two shillings was paid "for paynting of the Kingis armys, to be ane patroun to the broudstar".[3] On the death of Mary's father in 1542, "Johne Young brodister" was paid £21 10s. 0d. Scots for "brouderit wark wrought upon the coat of armes, furnessing gold and silk thairto" for the funeral.[4] Mary employed two professional embroiderers Pierre

Oudry and Ninian Miller, who appear to have worked throughout the whole of her time in Scotland, and another, Pier Veray, (though this may be a scribe's error for Pierre Oudry) who received the office of clerkship to "thair Majesties coquet and custumes of Edinburgh" on March 24th, 1566. In addition there were others not mentioned by name. There were listed in 1561 "fourty round sheittis quhilk servit to the broudinstaris that wrought upoun the tapestrie of the crammoisie velvois" as well as "ten single blankettis quhilkis servit the beddis of the brodinsters quha wrocht upoun the great pece of broderie" but it is not clear whether these worked for the Queen in France or in Edinburgh. "Ane tapestrie of heich cullourit crammoisie veluot maid in broderie quhilk is not yet compleit" (1561) appears never to have been finished and is docketed as "Brokin to make a claith of estait in anno 1566".[5]

The Queen also had three tapissiers (upholsterers) to provide furnishings for the court: Pierre Martin, Nicholas Carboneir, and one called David Liages. Her *valet de chambre*, Servais de Conde, had charge of all the 'moveables': beds, curtains, tapestries and linen that had belonged to her mother, and all those which the Queen had brought with her from France. He kept meticulous accounts, which are fortunately complete, of all those textiles given out which were not bought from merchants in Edinburgh. These latter were paid for by the Lord High Treasurer, some of whose accounts for these years are unfortunately missing. However, it is possible to build up a picture of the richness and variety of the silks, velvets, gold and silver thread and tissue and other materials used by the court during Mary's short stay.

She brought twenty-five beds and canopies, many of which were embroidered in appliqué with cloth of gold, together with eleven "auld Beddis" (which may have been in the palace when she arrived). From the time of her arrival new beds were constantly being made up and old ones renovated: for the Queen's ladies, for her female fool, Jardinière, for David Rizzio, and as wedding presents for members of her household. All the materials given out to the embroiderers and tapissiers were noted by the indefatigable Servais de Conde, even to "ung cartier de veloux noyr pour faire des collie au petit chien que la Royne ast envoye a France" in May 1564. Issues of velvet, silk, damask, taffetas, plaiding (plain, not tartan), cloth of gold, cloth of silver, passmenterie, gold and silver fringes, gold and silver thread are all recorded.

In addition, the Lord High Treasurer of Scotland disbursed money for the purchase of materials, silks and threads obtained from the merchants of Edinburgh, who must have rejoiced at the business brought by the Queen and her court. Even more must they have rejoiced when she married Darnley in 1565, for he ordered suits and armour without stint. The variety of materials and threads obtainable is surprising: "Poldavie canvas", a sailcloth used for tents and beds, small (perhaps narrow) canvas, white fustian, buckram, taffetas "of the six threads" and taffetas "of the four threads", "armosing taffetas", satin, velvet, holland cloth, Paris Black, gray black, "all hewis of worsate" (worsted) by the pound, silks of all colours by the ounce, sewing gold and silver by the pound, fine thread, coloured thread and "lincum twine" (strong enough to stitch mattresses), as well as on October 19th, 1562 "quhaill horne (whalebone) to be girds to the werdingallis" (farthingales).

At the end of May 1566, a splendid blue bed was made, apparently for the Queen's lying-in at the Castle, for which 115 ells of blue taffetas and $15\frac{1}{2}$ ells of blue velvet were bought for the canopy and curtains. This was trimmed with blue silk fringes and a gilded knob. Two tapestry covers were bought, though their use is not specified. Six stone of wool and six stone of feathers were used to stuff mattress and pillows. Ten ells of holland cloth (fine linen) were bought for the cradle, with ribbons, together with two hundred ells of the same material to be sarks (chemises or night-dresses) and sheets for the Queen. (A Scottish ell was 37 inches, 98·9 cms.)[6]

When the Queen was safely delivered of a son, the midwife, Margaret Asteane, was given material and thread to make a woollen gown of Paris black, trimmed with velvet. In the previous December the Queen's embroiderer, Pierre Oudry, had received as a gift a complete outfit of "Franche Black" cloak, doublet and hose trimmed with taffetas with a "marykin" (dressed goatskin) coat, and a fine hat costing forty shillings.[7] This gift, like that to the

16

midwife, must have been the reward for very personal service, such as drawing out the Queen's designs for embroidery and serving her in other ways. He eventually followed her into England in her captivity. A portrait of her painted at Sheffield in 1578 is ascribed to him.

For just over ten months she was imprisoned on Lochleven, from June 17th, 1567 to May 2nd, 1568, and it was only then that she would seem to have had the enforced leisure to embroider. Her well-known request to the Lords of the Council for "an imbroderer to drawe forthe such worke as she would be occupied with"[8] was clearly not granted, as being too dangerous, because her embroiderers, like Pierre Oudry, appear to have been faithful servants. She was strictly guarded and appears to have been allowed to take only two of her women.[9] Requests for her personal clothing and materials had to be sent to Edinburgh through her jailer.[10] The rather pathetic list of clothing and other items sent to her at Lochleven in July 1567 includes two pairs of leather and two pairs of velvet shoes, six hanks of twisted black Spanish silk, and several of other colours, a small crimson velvet casket with an F in silver gilt, which must have belonged to her first husband, (Francis II), another packet of smooth silks in assorted colours, and a dozen and a half of little flowers painted on canvas and outlined in black silk, together with "ung panne pleine de confiture". The little flowers on canvas were not, however, the "twa samplar peces pennit to be sewit" left by her mother when she died and handed to Servais de Conde in 1561. These were listed, still unworked, in Edinburgh Castle in 1578, ten years after Mary had left Scotland.

In August, as well as "une casset plein de confiture" there were sent pins, two ells of Holland cloth, two of lawn, a ball of soap for washing the hands, a packet of Spanish silks of all colours, and four hanks each of gold and silver thread. In September she wrote asking for twisted silk, if any remained, clothes for herself and her maidens "for thai are naikit", cambric, shoes, two pairs of sheets, gold, silver and black thread, covering for beds "to put under the tother covering", with prunes and pears.[11] In October Servais de Conde sent her most of the clothing requested, together with "des moulles et eguylle pour faire le reseu": netting needles and gauges to make knotted netting, perhaps to make 'cauls' or nets for their hair on that windy island.[12]

Since she was daily scheming for, and expecting, rescue, it is much more probable that she occupied herself with these small articles of needlework, than with the large hangings, now in the Royal Scottish Museum, which are believed to have come from Lochleven. The hangings are obviously professional work, requiring a large frame, and may have come from the royal workroom, for Lochleven was a royal castle. It was held by William Douglas by a licence signed by Mary and Darnley on November 13th, 1565 on condition "that the said house and place of Lochleven Castle salbe reddy and patent at thair Majesties commandment with all munition and artalliery being within the samyn . . . at quhatsumevir tyme thair hienessis sall pleis require the samyn upoun XXIIII houris warning".[13] She was, in fact, incarcerated in one of her own castles.

Beds and other furnishings had been sent from Edinburgh to all the royal residences, including Lochleven. A cloth of estate (the back and canopy for a royal chair) seized from Strathbogie, the house of the rebel Earl of Huntly in 1562 described as:

"6. Item, ane claith of estate of crammoisie satine figurat pirnit with gold furnisit with ruif, taill thre single pands (valances) the haill frengeit with gold and crammoisie silk.
— In Lochleven.

The hangings in the Royal Scottish Museum could easily have served as the back and valance for a chair of State, except that those described in the royal inventories appear to have been mounted on richer materials, velvet, silks or cloth of gold. These surviving hangings are of yellow silk embroidery mounted on to a red woollen cloth. In places where the appliqué has become detached, however, it is possible to see that the material had a short lustrous pile, and might have been mistaken when new for velvet by the clerk making the inventory.

Another hanging, so close in technique and material that it must have come from the same workshop, is also in the Royal Scottish Museum, and is believed to have come from Linlithgow,

18

Mary's birthplace. The royal inventory of 1561 lists two beds as being sent to Linlithgow, but no inventory of the furnishing there survives. Like the Lochleven hanging, it is worked in yellow silk on a red woollen ground and has lions of applied black velvet, crouching at the base of stylised trees (Plate 6).[14]

The design was a popular one in Scotland, an heraldic animal at the base of a tree which often had a bird in it. It appears on a bed valance made by Dame Julian Campbell between 1631–1640. The valance consists of a row of square panels, each with a tree or plant with an animal at the base (Plate 7). Uncut and unfinished motifs at Traquair, in fine tent stitch, prepared to be cut out and applied to another background, show the same type of design. Indeed, the griffin on one of them is identical with the griffin on the Campbell valance (Plate 8).

During Mary's long imprisonment in England, until her execution in 1587, she had all too much time for embroidery. There are many references, in letters and memoirs, to her activity with the needle, especially during the fifteen years she was in the custody of the redoubtable Countess of Shrewsbury and her husband.[15] Surprisingly, only two cushions at Hardwick, which was not built till after her death, and the panels showing her cypher, on the Oxburgh hangings in Norfolk, can be identified with certainty from the prodigious output of the Queen and her ladies over these years.

The four hangings of green velvet at Oxburgh Hall, Norfolk, the seat of the Bedingfield family, are thought to have come to Oxburgh through the Hon. Mary Browne, who married Sir Richard Bedingfield of Oxburgh in 1761, and who was descended from Anthony Browne, Lord Montague, a Catholic associate of the Earl of Shrewsbury, Mary's custodian. The hangings are regarded as Mary's work, not because of their history, but because the Queen's cipher, which occurs on her signet ring in the British Museum, and on her book stamp, is also to be found on several of the appliqué panels on the velvet hangings. These panels are worked in fine tent stitch or a coarser cross stitch. The cipher can also be seen on one of the two cushions at Hardwick Hall, ascribed to her. It is formed by the Greek letter ø for Francis II, Mary's first husband, and the letters MA. One of the Oxburgh panels has in

19

addition a large crowned monogram for MARIE STUART, flanked by thistles, surrounded by her motto-anagram: *"SA VERTU M'ATIRE"*. A central panel shows her cipher and the royal arms of Scotland, on either side of an emblem, a hand with a pruning hook cutting down a vine, with the motto *"Virescit Vulnere Virtus"* (Virtue flourishes by wounding). The cipher is found also on an octagonal panel which shows the marigold turning towards the sun, with the motto *NON INFERIORA SECUTUS* (Following no mean things) an emblem taken from C. Paradin, *Les Devises Heroiques* published at Lyons in 1557. This emblem, which occurs again on one of the larger panels, was the *impresa* of Mary's sister-in-law, Marguerite de Valois, the first wife of Henry of Navarre, but it can equally represent Mary's own motto-anagram *SA VIRTU M'ATIRE*. (Plate 9(a) and (b)). Other panels applied to the hangings show the initials of Elizabeth Shrewsbury (the E S which she had set like a crown above Hardwick Hall), and those of three of her four husbands.[16]

The panels are small enough to have been easily portable when stretched on a frame; the largest is not more than two feet square. The designs are well drawn. In England, unlike Lochleven, she was allowed her embroiderers, to draw out designs. As well as Pierre Oudry, whose name is on the Sheffield portrait of 1578, there is also a reference to a Charles Plouvart in 1586.[17] The choice of designs is intensely personal. Some of the birds and beasts were taken from *Historiae Animalium* published by C. Gesner in 1551, whose half-mythical animals served as pattern sources to decorators as well as needlewomen.[18]

The symbolism of the other panels, using *emblems*, those pictures with a Latin motto offering a moral thought or meditation, is today almost incomprehensible to us, even with an English translation of the motto. In the sixteenth century, emblems, and emblem books, from which some of these designs originate, were a part of the educated man's or woman's intellectual equipment. They were recognized and solved, just as some today enjoy solving recondite clues of crossword puzzles. Princes adopted an emblem as a personal symbol or *impresa*. Mary's mother took the phoenix with the motto *"En ma fin git mon commencement"* as her *impresa*. Amongst her daughter's beds was "ane bed of crammoisie veluot enrichit with phenixes of gold and tears" which was renovated in October 1566.

The remarkable bed described by William Drummond of Hawthornden, in his letter to Ben Jonson of July 1619 (see Appendix) as having been wrought and embroidered by Queen Mary, had her mother's emblem as well as Mary's own *impresa*: the lodestone turning to the Pole with her motto-anagram *SA VERTU M'ATIRE*. "This hath reference to a crucifix, before which with all her Royall ornaments she is humbled on her knees most lively with the word *Undique*." William Drummond writes with such detail and conviction that it is difficult not to believe that he had actually seen the bed. The embroideries on this bed may have been made by the Queen herself in France. It is, however, not recognizable in the inventories, unless it was "An bed of crammoisie broun veluot made in broderie work and leiffis of claith of gold with sum histories maid in the figure ovaill." The ovals may have contained emblems worked in fine tent stitch like the Oxburgh hangings. Or it may have been a black velvet one "enrichit with armes and spheris". This is recorded at Edinburgh Castle in 1578, but the first had by then disappeared, or else been moved to one of the other palaces for the use of James I. No trace of it now remains.

REFERENCES

1. FLEMING, D. H., *Mary Queen of Scots*, Hodder and Stoughton, London, 1897, p. 273.

2. See FLEMING, op. cit., pp. 515–43 for a daily list of her journeys during her reign of Scotland.

3. *Accounts of the Lord High Treasurer* (of Scotland), Vol. V, pp. 424–5.

4. *Accounts of the Lord High Treasurer*, Vol. VIII, p. 141.

5. *Inventaires de la Royne Descosse 1556–1569*, Bannatyne Club, no. III, Edinburgh, 1863, p. 38.

6. *Accounts of the Lord High Treasurer*, Vol. XI, p. 502.

7. *Accounts of the Lord High Treasurer*, Vol. XI, p. 446.

8. *Illustrations of the Reign of Queen Mary*, Maitland Club, Edinburgh, 1837, p. 220.

9. NAU, C., *History of Mary Stewart*, W. Paterson, Edinburgh, 1883, p. 260.

10. NAU, C., op. cit., p. 287

11. LABANOFF, A., *Lettres, Instructions et Memoires de Marie Stuart*, London, 1844, Vol. II, p. 61.

12. Papers from the Scots College, Paris, Maitland Club, 1834. *Moulle*: gauge or mesh for making nets.

13. *Registrum honoris de Morton*, Vol. I, Bannatyne Club, 1853, p. 12, no. 16.

14. See NEVINSON, J. L., *Burlington Magazine*, Vol. LXXVIII, April 1936, for a discussion of the origin of this design.

15. See WINGFIELD DIGBY, G., *Elizabethan Embroidery*, Faber and Faber, London, 1963 for an account of "Two Noble Needlewomen".

16. ZULUETA, F. DE, *Embroideries by Mary Stuart and Elizabeth Talbot at Oxburgh Hall, Norfolk*, Oxford, 1923.

17. WINGFIELD DIGBY, G., op. cit., p. 55.

18. APTED, M. R., *The Painted Ceilings of Scotland*, H.M.S.O., p. 33, ceiling at Earlshall, Leuchars, Fife.

Bed Valances

Of all articles of furniture, beds were the most important during the sixteenth and seventeenth centuries. They are usually listed first in any inventory. In the royal Scottish inventory of 1561, they are preceded only by the cloths of estate: the hanging and canopy over the royal throne. The state bed, for royalty or nobility, must have been an imposing affair with sumptuous hangings, a suitable stage for birth and death, and the furnishings, the tester and valances, the curtains, coverings, mattress and bolster, are often described in surprising detail.

The cold climate made bedhangings a necessity in Scotland. Beds with tester and valances occur in many Netherlandish paintings of the fourteenth century, especially in scenes of the Annunciation, with the Virgin's bed curtain neatly tied up at one corner. Four-poster beds remained in use in Scotland, and probably the north of England, well into the nineteenth century. Many of them still remain in the houses for which they were made.

The valances around the three sides of the roof of the bed (the fourth at the head was usually against the wall), could be richly decorated, and as they were stretched tight and lined, they survived long after the matching curtains had been worn out by the constant pulling to close and open them. In the inventory of 1561, of beds belonging to Mary Queen of Scots, and probably brought by her from France (her mother's beds are listed separately), are eleven "Beddis maid in Broderie" and a set of *pands* (valances) only, as well as three "passmentit beds" (trimmed with braid, or gold or silver lace), five plain beds of taffetas, velvet and damask, and

23

eleven "auld Beddis" made of old pieces of tapestry or sewed silk or worsted.

The embroidery on the valances shows the most poetical fancy: "Jennets and personages and branches of holly", "Phoenixes of gold and tears": (the emblems of her mother, Mary of Lorraine and her mother-in-law, Catherine de Medici, on a crimson velvet bed), "arms and spheres", "cyphers of A, enriched with leaves and branches of holly" (this was the "Bed of Amitie" for which 12 ells of violet taffeta were issued in October 1566 to make a bedcover), a bed of crimson velvet enriched with love knots and ♀♀ perhaps the cypher of her husband, Francis II; "pots full of flowers with broderie work of lang roundis callit ovaill, quhairin the histories are contenit", and a bed "maid in broderie work of gold of the historie of the Workis of Hercules".[1] All these beds were still in Edinburgh Castle in 1578, when her son was twelve years old, and the Queen was a captive in England. The Hercules bed was probably the one listed at Hampton Court in 1659, the last year of the Commonwealth: "One standing bedstead the furniture of needleworke being ye labours of Hercules cont: Tester, head cloth and double vallons" with a note "This bed brought out of Scotland".[2]

Many valances attributed to the sixteenth century survive, probably because they were not subject to the wear of the curtains, and remained undisturbed till the bed itself was taken down. Those of silk appliqué have mostly long ago disintegrated; those that are left, generally worked in woollen tent stitch (a half cross stitch on canvas), with silk highlights, are splendidly durable. Most of those with a known provenance are Scottish, some of them associated with Mary Queen of Scots. Scottish embroidered valances of this period fall into three main types:

1. Biblical subjects, obviously home-made.
2. Designs showing a tree with an heraldic animal crouching at the base, as in the Linlithgow hangings.
3. Tent stitch valances showing figures wearing French costume, with Biblical or mythological scenes, some of them exceedingly obscure. It is this type in particular which is associated with Mary Queen of Scots, chiefly on account of the costume.

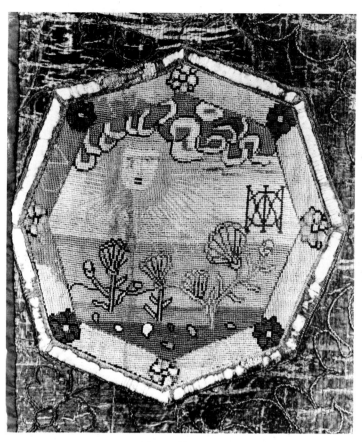

Plate 9 (a). Octagonal panel, one of several applied to a green velvet hanging, showing the cipher of Mary Queen of Scots (M A with Ø for Francis II of France, her first husband). The design, marigolds turning to the sun, with the motto NON INFERIORA SECUTUS was the emblem or *inpresa* of the sister of Francis, Marguerite de Valois, the first wife of Henry of Navarre. It also represents the anagram on the name Maria Stuart: *Sa virtu m'atire*. Coloured silks on canvas.

Tent and cross stitches. The panel is bordered by fragments of silk damask and looped gold wire. It is applied to green velvet decorated with scrolls of gold and red silk cord. About 43 cm. at its widest point. V. and A. T29–1955.

Oxburgh Hall on loan from the Victoria and Albert Museum

Plate 9 (b). Emblem from C. PARADIN *Devises Heroiques* Lyons 1557. NON INFERIORA SECUTUS. 11·5 × 7 cm.

Plate 10. Bed valance with initials CC KR. The initials and arms are those of Colin Campbell of Glenorchy and his second wife Katherine Ruthven whom he married in 1550. He died in 1585. One of a set of three from Balloch, now Taymouth Castle. The design shows the Temptation and Expulsion from the Garden of Eden, and appears to have been taken from a woodcut.
Coloured wools and silk on linen canvas. 1550–1585. The stitch is uncertain.
33 × 120·7 cm. no. 29 181.   *Burrell collection Glasgow Museum and Art Gallery*

Plate 11. The Arniston panel, perhaps a table carpet, with initials K O. The initials on either side of the arms resting on an elephant's howdah are those of Katherine Oliphant who married, as her second husband, George Dundas of that Ilk. She died in 1602. The upper medallion shows St. Paul urging Timothy to take a glass of wine: PAUL SAYING TO TEMOTHE THK A LYTL VYN TO COMFORT THY STO-MOK T5C, and below a gentleman gives a loaf to a beggar: THE LORD COMANDES THE TO BREAK YE BREAD AND GVE YT YE HOVNGRY SAM I 12. The wide border, which has been patched with fragments apparently taken from a similar panel is filled with flowers, fruit, vases and grotesque masks and fabulous monsters.
Coloured wools on linen. Stitch is the same as Plate 10. 213.4 × 91.4cm.
Trustees of the late Evelyn Henrietta Lady Dundas of Arniston, and Miss V.M.E. Dundas of Arniston

Plate 12. Detail from a set of three valances, now sewn together to form a panel. The valances are known to have come from Kilbryde Castle, Perthshire. The detail shows a strapwork medallion filled with flowers and fruit enclosing a quince tree with a bird in it; at the foot of the tree a stag crouches (compare this motif with plate 13, and with comparable motifs in Plates 7 and 8). Coloured wools and silks on canvas. Tent and cross stitches. Panel measures 121·9 × 167·6 cm.   *Mr. Eric J. Ivory*

Plate 13. Valance from a set of three (one missing) and two cushions showing the Five Senses. In this valance four panels, exclosed in strapwork containing flowers and fruit, have rural scenes with a flowering tree with birds in them. Left centre is a lady and gentleman with a peacock; right centre a lady with a mirror, symbolizing Sight, with a turkey. The animal attribute of Sight is generally depicted as an eagle, not a turkey.
Coloured wools, silks on canvas.
Tent stitch.   39·2 × 152·5 cm.   no. 1959 584.
Royal Scottish Museum

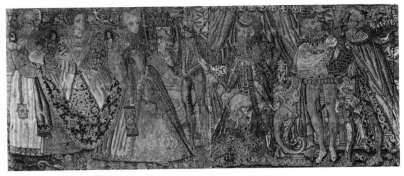

Plate 14. Valance, one of a pair from Murthly Castle, Perthshire. Solomon receiving the Queen of Sheba. The costumes are those of the French court 1574–1589, and are probably copied from prints of royal personages or courtiers. Coloured wools and silks on canvas. Tent stitch. 57.5 x 172.5cm. no.1905 1203.
Royal Scottish Museum

Plate 15. Fragment of a large hanging. Crewel work embroidery on cotton/
linen twill which is stamped on the back '1640 Bruges', presumably the mark
of the authorities of that city who had passed the cloth for sale. So-called
'Jacobean work'.
Coloured wools on linen/cotton twill.
Long and short and fishbone stitches.   33 × 40 cm.
The Earl of Elgin and Kincardine

Plate 16. Detail from a set of bedhangings, signed and dated M H 1699. The initials and crest are those of Margaret, daughter of the third Duke of Hamilton, who married the Earl of Panmure in 1687. She died in 1731.
Silk and gold on linen quilted with yellow silk.
Back, stem and satin stitches, and laid gold work. 45·7 × 36 cm.

Lady Broun Lindsay

Plate 17. Portion of a bed valance on fine linen. Acorns and carnations.
Early 18th. century.
Coloured silks on linen.
Long and short and filling stitches.   30 × 170 cm.
The Earl of Haddington

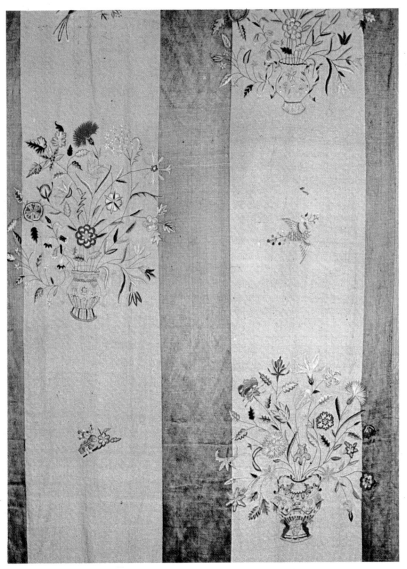

Plate 18. Detail of a bed curtain, dated 1729, one of a set of four, dated respectively 1727, 1728, 1729 and 1730. They were worked by Janet, daughter of Colonel Francis Charteris, who married James, 4th Earl of Wemyss in 1720. Each curtain has her initials and those of her husband incorporated into a vase of the design, together with those of her children as they were born.

Coloured silk embroidery on fine linen 63·5 cm. wide, with blue satin stripes. Satin, stem, long and short and cross stitches. 241·3 × 123·2 cm.

Captain Michael Wemyss

BED VALANCES

The first section is the best documented. Probably the earliest of the home-made valances is the set of three now in the Burrell Collection, Glasgow, showing the arms and initials of Sir Colin Campbell of Glenorchy, and of his second wife, Katharine Ruthven, whom he married in 1550. He died in 1583, and since she was a second wife it may be assumed that the valances were made soon after their marriage in 1550. All three valances show the Campbell of Glenorchy arms: the shortest, at the foot of the bed, shows them impaling the Ruthven arms, with a true lover's knot between the initials C.C. and K.R. suspended from a ram's head, the Ruthven supporter. On either side are lively scenes of the *Temptation of Adam and Eve*, and the *Expulsion from Paradise*. The drawing of the figures, though crude, has great vitality, and suggests that they were taken from woodcuts in an early printed book or Bible, many of which show these two scenes. But the Devil in the tree is distinctive, with his serpent's tail, human head and clawed hands. The other two valances show motifs which could equally have been taken from title pages or headings of printed books: mermaids, winged putti or cupids astride a branch, the lion and unicorn, and exotic flowers.

The most remarkable and interesting thing about these valances is the stitch employed. It is not tent stitch, but at first glance appears to be chain stitch. However, an examination of the back, shows that instead of the vertical line of stitches which occurs in chain stitch, the stitches occur in pairs, horizontally. They appear to have been worked in two journeys, the needle held horizontally, producing a V-shaped stitch on the right side. This is a very rapid way of covering the canvas, and the colours are worked in vertical stripes, imitating the hatching of a woven tapestry. (Plate 10.) The stitch bears a striking resemblance to the background stitch of a red silk panel of the same period at Hardwick, decorated with vertical rows of oak leaves. But the Hardwick panel is very clearly long-armed cross stitch, with double, not single, horizontal stitches at the back.

The same stitch occurs on another Scottish embroidery of the same period: a panel at Arniston, Midlothian, with the initials K.O. and arms of Oliphant resting on an elephant's howdah. The

25

initials are those of Katherine Oliphant, who married before 1565 her second husband, George Dundas, seventeenth Laird of Dundas and first of Arniston. The border of the panel has been repaired with fragments of a similar hanging, but the size and inscriptions of the centre panel strongly suggest that it was originally a table carpet. There are two oval medallions, one where St. Paul urges Timothy to take a glass of wine: PAUL SAYING TO TEMOTHE THK A LYTL VYN TO COMFORT THY STOMOK, and another, where a gentleman with flat cap and a gown with slashed sleeves gives loaves to a beggar: THE LORD COMMANDS THE TO BREAK YE BREAD AND GYE YT YE HOVNGRY. (Plate 11.) In addition to being worked in the same stitch as the Campbell valances, their border designs have many other features in common, especially in the exotic flowers and fruit.

Another home-made set of valances of Scottish origin is in the Metropolitan Museum, New York. They came from Balhousie Castle, Perth,[3] and may, indeed, be related to the Campbell of Glenorchy set, for although these valances were acquired from the family of Hay of Kinnoul, who were granted Balhousie in 1625, the castle had before that belonged to the Earl of Gowrie, head of the Ruthven family, who was killed and his estates confiscated after the Gowrie conspiracy in 1600. These valances also show a story of Adam and Eve, surrounded, as in the Arniston panel, by borders of fruit, birds, and grotesque figures. Tent stitch is used for the flesh, the robes of God are of applied silk, and the greater part of the background is described as chain stitch. The figures in the six incidents illustrated have all been identified by Mrs. Cabot[4] as coming from the small woodcuts of Bernard Salomon (1508–1561) illustrating *Quadrins historiques de la Bible* published by Jean de Tourmes, Lyons, in 1553. Only the figures are copied from the woodcuts, and have been placed in a background of birds, flowers and animals, reminiscent of an earlier woven tapestry. Although the figures lack the elegant mannerism of the Salomon woodcuts, they are well drawn on the canvas by a draughtsman who gave the scenes added drama by making the figures appear to step out of their frame by drawing the hands and feet overlapping the border.

Another home-made valance, also in the Metropolitan Museum belongs to the second group; those that show a tree with an heraldic animal crouching at the foot, as in the Linlithgow hanging. This valance, which has already been referred to (Plate 7), was also made by the wife of a Campbell of Glenorchy, in this case, by Dame Julian Campbell of Loudon Castle, Ayrshire, who married Sir Colin Campbell of Glenorchy (1577–1640),[5] grandson of Katherine Ruthven whose arms are on the Burrell valance. This second Campbell valance must have been made between 1631, when Sir Colin succeeded his father as Laird of Glenorchy, and 1640 when he died.

Yet another set of valances shows the design of a tree with a bird in it with an animal crouching at the foot. It has now been made into a single panel and came from Kilbryde Castle, Perthshire[6] (Plate 12). In this embroidery, the tree and animal are enclosed in strapwork filled with fruit. This is a professional piece, well drawn, and excellently worked in tent stitch. Until 1643, Kilbryde Castle, from which the valance came, belonged to the Earls of Mentieth. The 4th Earl, John, accompanied the child, Queen Mary, to France in 1550. The valance may have been acquired in France, as it has certain similarities in design to one in the Victoria and Albert Museum which belonged to Louis de Farcy, the French writer on needlework. In 1587, the 6th Earl of Mentieth married Mary, a daughter of Sir Colin Campbell of Glenorchy and Katherine Ruthven, so that this valance also has some connexion with the Campbell valances.

Yet another set of valances showing trees with birds set in panels of strapwork is in the Royal Scottish Museum, Edinburgh. Their provenance is unknown, but may have been Scottish. In this set are two valances (one missing) and two cushions or pillows in tent stitch. Each piece has figures depicting one of the *Five Senses* (*Taste* is missing) (Plate 13). This set links the 'tree' design with what is the largest and most complicated known group of valances: those that show figures wearing a fashionable French costume of the late sixteenth century.

These valances usually depict Biblical or mythological scenes, but they are often extremely difficult to identify. The principal actors are wearing stiff and elaborate clothes, drawn and embroidered in great detail, in courtly surroundings with canopied thrones, or formal gardens with fountains. The incidents succeed each other along the valances in the manner of a strip cartoon. In Scotland they are often associated with Mary Queen of Scots, and though she obviously did not make them herself, it is often assumed that they were brought by her from France, or were made in Edinburgh during her reign in Scotland. This assumption is probably based on the fact that most of them come from families known to have been close to the Queen. A striking set belonging to Lord Forbes shows the story of Leto and Artemis from Ovid's *Metamorphoses*. Two in the Royal Scottish Museum came from Murthly Castle, Perthshire; they belonged to Sir William Stuart, who was page to Mary's son, (James I and VI) and was brought up with the Prince. One of the valances shows Solomon receiving the Queen of Sheba (Plate 14), and is reminiscent of Bernard Salomon's woodcut of the subject. Another set with unidentified topic belonged to the Earls of Morton who were descended from Sir William Douglas of Lochleven.[7] The Duke of Buccleuch owns a single valance showing Daniel being raised from the lions' den. Yet another, now destroyed, showed the story of Rehoboam, and is known to have been in Edinburgh since the seventeenth century. It was thought to have been one mentioned in the Royal inventories, but this theory has now been discredited.[8] One of the minor incidents depicted on this set, the *Disobedient Prophet* of I Kings XIII 11–28, used as a background detail, is taken from the incident illustrated by Bernard Salomon in *Quadrins historiques de la Bible*.

The nationality of these valances, and the source of their involved designs, have remained unsolved problems. Individual figures, such as the *Disobedient Prophet* with the lion and ass, have been traced to a printed source. A large table carpet or coverlet in the same style, showing *Lucretia's Banquet*, in the Victoria and Albert Museum (T125–1913) was identified by C. E. C. Tattersall as deriving from an engraving by Philippe Galle (1537–1612). Mrs. Cabot has traced the origin of a number of figures on valances in the Victoria and Albert Museum and in other collections, and has found that most of them came from printed Bible illustrations, notably those by Bernard Salomon also from the *Antiquitates Judaicae*, Frankfort, 1580, illustrated by Jost Amman, and the *Thesaurus Sacrarum*, Antwerp, 1585 of Gerard de Jode.

It would appear that the designers of these valances, who were, perhaps, not skilled in figure drawing, had before them sheets of these engravings, from which they copied one or a group of figures. The classical draperies worn by the characters in the engravings were changed to a sumptuous highly detailed French court costume, probably copied from other prints, and the background filled in with landscapes and buildings to the designer's own, or his patron's, taste. This assumption is considerably strengthened by the existence of two valances illustrating the same subject: both allegories of a man choosing between the three cardinal Virtues and the Sensual world. One valance is in the Ashmolean museum, Oxford, and the other, on loan to the Victoria and Albert Museum, belongs to Miss Maud Ochs. Their arrangement is very similar. In both cases on the left stand Faith, Hope and Charity, but in different positions and wearing different clothes in each version. To the right the same single male figure appears on each, a man with a forked beard, leaning on a staff. In the *Disobedient Prophet* group on the Rehoboam valances, the draughtsman has rearranged the position of the lion and the ass, though keeping closely to Bernard Salomon's drawing of each figure. The costumes shown in this group of valances, drawn in sumptuous detail, would appear to have been copied from French fashion plates, but so far none of these plates has been identified.

The Bible engravings were freely available in Protestant as well as Catholic countries all over Europe, and, with these scenes to serve as models, there is no reason why valances found in Scotland should not have been made there. It is highly improbable that they were made during Mary's brief stay in her kingdom, or that they were brought by her from France. The beds in the inventories, and those for which material was given out or bought, appear all to have had valances decorated with appliqué in cloth of gold, silk or gold embroidery, but not made in worsted tent stitch. Worsted was bought, but appears to have been used to repair existing tapestries or needlework. On two occasions, two (not three as would be required for valances) "cuverings of tapestrie" were provided for beds, once for the Queen's lying-in, and once for the nursery of the infant prince at Stirling Castle in 1566.[9] In 1578, after the Queen had left Scotland, there were still, at Edinburgh Castle, "certane werklumes (large frames) for ane brodinstare" and, amongst all the pieces of gold and silver embroidery "a pand (valance) of cammes drawn upon paper and begun to sew with silk".

All the available evidence suggests that these tent-stitch valances with figures in elaborate French clothes belong to a slightly later date than 1568, when Mary left Scotland. Indeed, the costumes on most of them confirm this,[10] and the only dated example of this style of needlework is 1594.[11] But the surviving Scottish examples could still have been made in Edinburgh during the reign of Mary's son: the families who owned them were closer to him than to his mother, as for instance was Sir William Stuart, owner of Murthly Castle. One set of valances, now belonging to Lord Glentanar, was originally owned by the Earls of Morton, descended from Sir William Douglas of Lochleven, Mary's custodian there. But Sir William's grandson, William, Earl of Morton, was a devoted servant of both James and his son, Charles I, and became one of the richest men in the kingdom. Not all of Mary's embroiderers left Scotland when the Queen departed. Ninian Miller was still working in Edinburgh in 1583, as was the King's embroiderer, William Beaton.

In spite of the large number of Scottish tent-stitch valances, with their strong French flavour, there is no evidence that the fashion originated in Scotland. No doubt the climate there made them more acceptable, but tent-stitch valances, with designs from engraved sources, are also to be found in France and Germany. It was an international fashion that could be adapted, like so many needlework designs, to the taste of each country.

BED VALANCES

REFERENCES

1. *Inventaires de la Royne Descosse*, 1556–1569, Bannatyne Club, Edinburgh, no. 111, 1863, p. 31, no. 18. There was also a *tapestry* of the works of Hercules, containing 8 pieces, p. 39, no. 88.

2. LAW, E., *Hampton Court*, Vol. II, George Bell & Sons, London, 1888, p. 285.

3. STANDEN, E., "Two Scottish embroideries in the Metropolitan Museum," *Connoisseur*, Vol. CXXXIX, 1957, p. 196.

4. CABOT, N. G., "Pattern Sources of Scriptural subjects in Tudor and Stuart embroideries," *Bulletin of the Needle and Bobbin Club*, New York, Vol. 30, 1946, p. 3.

5. STANDEN, E., op. cit., p. 196.

6. Now in the collection of Eric J. Ivory, Esq., Edinburgh.

7. Now in the collection of Lord Glentanar, Aboyne.

8. SCOTT MONCRIEFF, R., *Proceedings of the Society of Antiquaries of Scotland*, 1918, p. 72.

9. FLEMING, D. H., *Mary Queen of Scots*, 1897, p. 500.

10. I am grateful to Mr. John L. Nevinson for confirming this.

11. Christie's sale, July 9th, 1931, Lot 57.

5

Bed Curtains and Hangings

We do not know what curtains hung beneath the tent-stitch valances; they have perished or have been cut up long ago. But in 1640 the valance made soon after 1550 by Katherine Ruthven (Plate 10) was still apparently on a bed at Balloch (now Taymouth Castle) the home of the Campbells of Glenorchy. Among other beds listed, with the Campbell arms embroidered and applied to valances of velvet, silk and "London cloth", there was "ane vther silk bed of changing taffite greine and yellow, conteining IIII curtaines, quhairof iii of Spanische taffite and ane of cesnat (sarcenet) taffite, with ane pand (valance) schewit with silk and worsett with the Laird and Lady Glenvrquhy thair names and airmes thairon, with ane grein silk fass conteining ii pece with ane covering wrought with blue and yellow silk".[1]

Although this sounds rather startling beneath valances depicting the Temptation and Expulsion, the green and yellow shot taffeta curtains with a blue and yellow bedcover would have accorded well with the colours of the valances, which are worked mainly in three or four shades of indigo with black outlines, with some fawn and brown and a little red, picked out with silk highlights of yellow, green and a purple-pink.[2]

But by 1679 the valances were stored away in a chest.[3] For a new and lighter fashion in bed curtains had been adopted, even in Scotland, by the middle of the seventeenth century. Silks were expensive, and in the war-torn years of that period were often difficult to import. Instead, a material of linen and cotton with a twill weave was used, decorated in a variety of stitches with bold leafy designs in coloured worsteds, often described without much foun-

Plate 19. Needlework picture. Abraham entertaining the Angels.
Coloured wools and silks on canvas. Late 17th. century.
Fine tent stitch.   49·5 × 48·2 cm.   no. 1945. 1550.
Royal Scottish Museum

Plate 20. Engraving by Gerard de Jode. Abraham entertaining the Angels from *Thesaurus Sacrarum Historiaru Veteris Testamenti* Antwerp 1585. 19 × 28 cm.

Plate 21. The Mellerstain Panel, signed and dated G B R B M M 1706. The initials are those of Grisell Baillie, born 1692, Rachel Baillie, her sister born 1696, and May Menzies, their governess. All the motives are taken from *A Booke of Beast, Birds, Flowers, Fruits, Flies and Wormes*, . . . published by *Thomas Johnson at Brittayne's Burse* (the Exchange) 1630. The centrepiece of the panel is copied from the engraving *Smelling* showing a woman with a bunch of flowers and a dog, the animal attribute of the sense of smell. This is one of the set of the *Five Senses* bound into the volume. The flowers and animals have all been chosen from different pages of the book.

Coloured wools and silks on a blue ground on canvas.

Fine tent stitch.   33 × 49·5 cm.

The Earl of Haddington

Plate 22. Engraving. *Smelling* from the *Five Senses*. Engraver unidentified. Bound into the Mellerstain copy of Thomas Johnson's *A Booke of Beast* . . . the vellum binding of which is impressed K L for Katherine Logan, whose signature and the date 1635 is inside the binding. Katherine Logan was the grandmother of May Menzies, governess to the two daughters of Lady Grisell Baillie, Grisell and Rachel.

The Earl of Haddington

Plate 23. Page from *A Booke of Beast* . . . published by Thomas Johnson in 1630. The marigold and olives are copied from *Hortus Floridus* by Crispin van de Passe, published in Arnhem 1614, and have been traced directly on to the canvas. The group with the peacock, fox and porcupine appear at the top of the panel. The marigold, reversed, is top left, the olives below.

The Earl of Haddington

dation, as 'Jacobean'. No examples are known as early as the reign of James VI and I, who died in 1625, though they must still have been fashionable in the short reign of his grandson, James II (1685–1688). The branching leaves and exotic flowers are often thought to have been copied from the printed and painted cotton hangings imported by the East India Company, but Mr. John Irwin has suggested,[4] instead, that these were supplied in large quantities from India in response to a European demand for 'branches' and verdure indoors: a kind of garden room decoration.

Wool embroidery on linen was not, of course, an innovation. The embroidery on that long strip that we call the Bayeux tapestry is embroidered in wools on a linen background. Silks for needle-work were always expensive, since they had to be imported from Mediterranean countries, and so we find in Germany, wall hangings of linen worked in wools of bright colours were made during the fourteenth and fifteenth centuries. A striking example at Regens-burg dating from about 1370 has amusing medallions showing the wiles of women, and is worked in thick worsted, with a brick-red tied stitch background, very like the stitch on the Bayeux tapestry. Medieval Regensburg was a centre of the linen trade in southern Germany, but it is understandable that woollen thread, rather than linen, was used for the decoration of the wall hanging, since wool accepts dyestuffs more readily than flax, and will dye to more brilliant shades.

Trade, politics and religion drew Scotland closely to the Low Countries during the seventeenth century. Holland and Scotland shared the Calvinist religion. The University of Edinburgh, the first Protestant university to be founded after the medieval establish-ments of St. Andrews, Glasgow and Aberdeen, followed closely the teaching of that of Leiden. Scottish merchants from east coast ports, from Aberdeen to Leith, exported wool, coal, skins and fish, and brought back timber from the Baltic, linen, laces and wine. The Scottish Staple at the port of Veere in Holland, where the Scots enjoyed many privileges, was the main link. One of the most sub-stantial merchants in this trade was James Bruce of Culross (died 1625). His descendants still possess fragments of large hangings, probably bed curtains, worked in crewels (twisted worsted) on a twill cotton/linen ground, stamped "1640 Bruges", perhaps imported by his son, Sir George Bruce, who died in 1643.[5] (Plate 15.)

There are, as yet, no records available of an extensive manufacture of this twilled cloth in Bruges, but the city had been a textile centre for centuries, and the Dutch East India Company, which could have supplied the cotton, then only available from India, was founded in 1602. The contemporary name of the cloth is not known; it may have been dimity or fustian, both of which are recorded in association with crewel embroidery. A letter in the Verney Memoirs of 1663 refers to "a Dimity bed in green crewels".[6] We have not, so far, any evidence of the twill being manufactured in Britain. Bruges had furnished the symbolism, and perhaps the linen, for the Fetternear Banner; now it furnished the material for a secular embroidery. Trade still flourished, in spite of the split in religion.

These hangings are the earliest known examples of *crewel work* to survive. A workbag dated 1660, and another in the Victoria and Albert dated 1672 (T.394–1912) together with some fragments dated 1680 in the Basingstoke Museum, and a pair of curtains dated 1696 in the Royal Ontario Museum, Toronto (961–120), seem to be the only dated pieces. So many of these crewel work curtains, or fragments of them, still remain that it is irresistible to suppose that it was a widespread fashion spreading over a longer period. Like the tent-stitch valances, they may owe their survival to the durability of the material, though in some instances the embroidery has been carefully cut out and remounted on to another linen.

The 6th Earl of Morton, a devoted servant of James VI and I and grandson of Sir William Douglas of Lochleven, was made Earl of Orkney in 1643. His wife, Agnes Keith, died in Kirkwall, Orkney, in May 1648. Her husband died in August, and her son, who succeeded him, died a year later. In all this upheaval, her belongings were carefully preserved by one of her maids, and listed methodically in March 1650. Amongst her belongings was a white fustian bed, "sow'd with Incarnat worsett", but the list contains many items of such interest that they deserve to be included here:

34

BED CURTAINS AND HANGINGS

Compt of the Wardropy Sometym in the Custody of Besse Webb, Servitour to the Noble Laydy Morton. 11 March 1650.

... 1 Gryt Sweet Bagg soad with pitty point.

   1 Gryt Sweet Bagg Imbrodered with silber and gold.

   1 littl Whyt Box with Purling with ane Number of other small things therin.

... 3 Sweet Baggs Imbroded with gold and silver of Taffety.

   1 pound and half of new Collord Silk.

   $\frac{1}{2}$ pund of Sowing gold besides old Collours of Silk.

1 Trunk containing therin

   1 Whyt fustan bedd, sow'd with Incarnat worsett wheroff 15 pieces was of it.

   4 pieces of Galls great and small.

   1 little brod box with ane Dosson ells of blak and gold Ribbons therein.

   1 little Flanders Basket wrought with ane wowen silk Kusshon therin unmead up.

   1 pund and half new Collord silk.

   $\frac{1}{2}$ pund of sowing gold, besyds old cullors of silk. (in another chest).

   1 gryt wooddin cabinett with Shottles containing therin.

   $\frac{1}{2}$ Book of Gold.

   $\frac{1}{2}$ stone of collord worsett.

   $\frac{1}{2}$ pound of small Naples Silk of all cullors.

   $\frac{1}{2}$ pound Ingram'd worsett.

Summe other sind (things?).

   2 Dosson fox skinns.

   18 Shambo skinns.

   1 Barroll of Black Woll.

   1 Extraordinary great Glas in a box of Sweetwood, showing the half of the Boddy.

   6 Gryt Bybles.

   1 Sowing book of all cullors guylded, with gold on the cover.[7]

This is a remarkable collection of imported articles to be found in a castle in the Orkneys in the seventeenth century. The mirror that caused so much amazement reminds us that silvered glass was a new manufacture in the seventeenth century. Some of the six great Bibles may have had illustrations that would serve as models for needlework panels. The "sowing Book" is a tantalizing mystery. Although it was not listed among the personal possessions of the Countess, the family were probably the owners also of the set of valances (see page 28), now belonging to Lord Glentanar.

Crewel work was not the only adornment for bed hangings in the seventeenth century; they were made in a variety of styles. As we have seen, the Campbells of Glenorchy in 1640 had curtains of silk, curtains of red London cloth with black velvet appliqué, and green London cloth decorated with green and orange silk braid. At Blair Castle there is a handsome bed which came from Charlotte de la Trémouille, mother of the first Duchess of Atholl. She was the intrepid Countess of Derby, who successfully withstood a siege of several months by Cromwell's troops in her house at Lathom, Lancashire, while her husband, Governor of the Isle of Man, was absent. The bed at Blair Castle has white silk curtains and valances ornamented with fine *slips* of tent stitch in silk : motifs, including female figures of the Four Continents, which were worked on canvas and cut out to apply to a background of another material. The many unused panels of motifs of tent stitch at Traquair were intended to be used in just such a manner, and there is a bed at Hardwick decorated with them. Slips or motifs of this type applied to eighteenth-century yellow silk brocade decorate the walls of a room at Lennoxlove. They must have been placed there after 1702, for the house was rebuilt according to the wish of Frances Stuart (*La Belle Stuart*) Duchess of Richmond and Lennox, after her death in that year.

A handsome set of bed curtains worked in Florentine stitch in shades of green and cream silk, belonged to the Duke of Monmouth, son of Charles II, and descended to the Duke of Buccleuch, but they have since been cut and used to cover William and Mary walnut chairs.[8]

Pieces of a set of bed hangings dated 1699 show the Hamilton crest, an oak tree penetrated transversely in the main stem by a saw, and the motto THROUGH. They bear the initials M H for

Margaret Hamilton, a notable Jacobite, daughter of the third Duke of Hamilton. In 1687 she married the 4th Earl of Panmure. The crest and initials are worked in coloured silks and gold on a background of what appears to be fine linen, but may be cotton, quilted finely in an ellipitical design with yellow silk. This embroidery is superimposed on the quilting (Plate 16).

Finely quilted linen or cotton, often worked in yellow silk, forms the background of a great many sets of bed hangings or bedcovers of the eighteenth century. Sometimes the quilting is worked in small lozenges; occasionally it is a tightly worked random design. It may be found in bed hangings, valances, bedcovers or clothing, particularly petticoats.

Although there is as yet no documentary evidence to support the theory, it might perhaps be that as the yellow silk of the quilted ground is reminiscent of the yellow *muga* silk of Indian embroidery, the material may have been imported ready quilted from India for the needlewoman to add coloured embroidery of her own choice. This supposition is strengthened by two entries in the accounts of Lady Grisell Baillie:

London Jan. 1st. 1717. Account of my own Cloathes
    For 27 yd. white Indian Quilting at 4*s.* 6*d.* and
      5*s.* 6*d.* (stg.)   £4 13 6
. . . Account of my Rachy's cloath
    For 7 yards of Indian quilting at 5*s.* 6*d.*   £1 18 6
But at the same time:
    For a white satine quilted coat   £2 15 0[9]

The quilting on the coat would need to be worked after the separate parts had been marked out, and would therefore have to be done to order, and not bought by the yard.

It must not be thought, however, that crewel work or quilted bed hangings and coverlets were no longer made after the end of the seventeenth century, nor indeed that all the embroidered bed hangings were home-made. In 1652 Sir Ralph Verney of Claydon sent to his friend Dr. Morley in Antwerp for some embroidery for a bed. The lining, fringing and embroidery of two extra curtains cost him £30 sterling.[10] In 1683 Lady Forbes left her daughter "a web of green stamped cloth for bed hangings", but in spite of the new fashion, in Britain, and in colonial America, needlewomen continued to decorate linen, twill and quilted cotton bed hangings and covers with designs in crewels and silks until the end of the eighteenth century. Those that remain are often powdered with sprays of flowers, sometimes remarkably old-fashioned, reminiscent of the flowers in the much-pricked copy in the British Museum of *La Clef des Champs* published by Jacques le Moyne at Blackfriars in 1596. A set at Blair Castle, apparently made during the eighteenth century, using fine crewels, have the borage flower and strawberry plant, illustrated in woodcuts and engravings of the late sixteenth century.

Curiously, although a good many of these embroidered bed hangings still survive, the valances are often missing, perhaps because, unlike the tent-stitch valances, they may have suffered damage when it was necessary to take them down for washing. A splendid fragment in brilliant silks, with a deeply cut scalloped border, shows how colourful and vivid these lighter valances must have been (Plate 17).

The most beautiful set of four curtains still used on a bed must surely be those at Wemyss Castle, Fife, worked by Janet, Lady Wemyss, dated respectively 1727, 1728, 1729 and 1730, with the initials of her children, as they were born, over these years. They are worked in fine silks, with the ever-popular "potts of flowers" of Queen Mary's time, and Chinoiserie birds delicately embellishing a fine linen woven with blue satin stripes about 10 cm. wide. Unlike the bold initials on the Campbell valances, or those of Bess of Hardwick flaunted against the skyline above her house, the initials of the Countess and her children and husband (with whom, alas, she quarrelled) are hidden on each curtain, disguised as the pattern on one of the pots of flowers (Plate 18). Only one or two motifs are used, and are repeated in different colours.

This love of variety for its own sake, in colours, or in stitches as in the crewel work curtains, is characteristic of all domestic embroidery in Britain, as if the needlewoman were obliged to relieve the tedium of working a large piece by trying the effect of a new colour combination, or a new stitch. Even small pieces, such as needlework pictures, or raised work pictures and boxes, display this endearing idiosyncrasy.

REFERENCES

1. INNES, C. [ed.], *The Black Book of Taymouth*, Bannatyne Club, Edinburgh, 1855, p. 349.

2. A fragment of the purple-pink silk, kindly analysed by the Research Dept., Imperial Chemical Industries, Ltd. by permission of William Wells, Esq., Keeper of the Burrell Collection, shows evidence of being dyed with Kermes.

3. Breadalbane Papers, Box 22/4. Register House, Edinburgh.

4. IRWIN, J., "Origins of the 'Oriental Style' in English Decorative Art," *Burlington Magazine*, XCVII, 1955, p. 106.

5. I am indebted to the Countess of Elgin and Kincardine for information about this dated hanging.

6. *Memoirs of the Verney Family*, Longmans Green, London, 1925, Vol. II, p. 211.

7. Morton Papers, Box 156, no. 14, Register House, Edinburgh.

8. I am indebted to the Duchess of Buccleuch for this information.

9. *The Household Book of Lady Grisell Baillie*, Scottish History Society, 1911, pp. 208 and 214.

10. VERNEY, M. M., *Memoirs of the Verney Family*, Longmans Green, 1925, Vol. II, p. 487.

6

Needlework Pictures

Because so many of them have survived from the seventeenth century onwards, it is tempting to believe that small needlework pictures were a new development at that date. However, since the earliest times, the human figure has been embroidered on textiles. The nomad's head from Noin-Ula, the saints on St. Cuthbert's stole, the Normans and Saxons on the Bayeux tapestry, and the stiff courtly French figures of the tent-stitch valances are all richly pictorial. The little seventeenth-century panels that remain in such numbers differ in that they are home-made and intimate, intended merely as a domestic decoration. Most of them owe their survival to the fact that they were framed and glazed, and consequently have been preserved from dust and moth, though not, alas, from fading. The brilliant, almost garish, colours of the worsteds and silks are only perceived if the pictures are taken from their frames and the back of the work examined. Their small size is due, perhaps, to the fact that they were not too tedious to make and often were undertaken by children.

They are small domestic versions of woven tapestry, and the subjects chosen were those already popular in tapestries and valances: the *Five Senses*, the *Four Seasons* and the *Four Continents*. Mythological subjects are rare, but Old Testament heroines such as Esther, Susanna, Jephtha's daughter and Miriam, were particular favourites. In a Protestant country, figures of Christ and the saints were still, during a century torn by bitter religious wars, to be regarded as 'images', but a heroine of the Old Testament, like Esther, could be accepted as a symbol of a persecuted minority: such as the Royalists under the Commonwealth, the Puritans under James II,

and the Jacobites under William III and the Hanoverians. Remarkably, these Old Testament heroines also kept their popularity
in Catholic countries, where Esther, for instance, was used by
Baroque preachers as a prototype of Our Lady interceding for fallen
humanity. Susanna and the elders, which to the medieval preacher
symbolized the Church assailed by the forces of the Jews and the
Pagans, was to a Protestant the symbol of Virtue wrongly accused,
but to both it offered a delightful opportunity to portray the female
nude.

The needlewoman of the seventeenth century was certainly influenced in her choice of subject by the vast number of engravings,
executed mainly by Flemish or Dutch artists, especially of Biblical
subjects, that were available in print sellers' and booksellers' shops.
As in the tent-stitch valances, a figure or group of figures from one
of these engravings was drawn on to the canvas, but clothed, once
more, in a rich court costume. An entirely different landscape was
usually added, complete with fishponds, flowers, birds, beasts and
caterpillars wholly out of proportion to the human figures and each
other, which today we find amusing and irrational. A great deal of
work has been done on the engraved sources of these embroideries,
notably by Mr. J. L. Nevinson[1] and Mrs. Nancy Groves Cabot.[2] It is
now possible to recognize the main origins of these designs, and to
dispose of the myth that the needlewoman created her own by
copying the flowers and birds she saw in her own garden. The Old
Testament scenes, as in the case of the valances, came from the
enormously popular Bible illustrations of Bernard Salomon (1508–
1561), Jost Amman (1539–1591) and Gerard de Jode (1531–
1591). The last named published, in 1585 in Antwerp, *Thesaurus
Sacrarum Historiarū Veteris Testamenti*, a volume of oblong
quarto plates with Latin texts, that must have been widely used, for
needlework versions of his engravings occur in many guises, according to the skill and technique of the needlewoman. His version of
Abraham entertaining the angels, for instance, can be found in the
Royal Scottish Museum (1945–4550) (Plate 19), the Untermyer
Collection in New York[3] and in the Victoria and Albert Museum
(443–1865). De Jode's version of Abraham banishing Hagar and
Ishmael can be found in the picture in the Burrell collection **(B.41)**,

the Victoria and Albert raised work picture (125–1878) and the unfinished mirror frame (247–1896), as well as one in the collection of Mrs. Myron C. Taylor, U.S.A. Indeed, Mrs. Cabot has identified no less than thirteen extant embroideries in Britain and the United States taken from this engraving alone (Plate 20).

Inevitably, English publishers and engravers in London found how useful and popular printed sheets of engravings could be, not only as illustrations in books, but as pattern designs for craftsmen of all types, sculptors, metal and glass engravers as well as the domestic embroideress. Mr. J. L. Nevinson has described the publications of various London printsellers of the seventeenth century. Thomas Johnson published in 1630 *A Booke of Beast [sic], Birds, Flowers, Fruits, Flies and Wormes, exactly drawne with their Lively Colours truly Described* (B.M. 462.b.18). These were plates, that could apparently be purchased singly, with engravings borrowed from a variety of sources. The flowers came from the *Hortus Floridus* of Crispin van de Passe, published in Arnhem in 1614. Other flowers, and some of the fruit, as well as the flies and caterpillars, were taken from the beautiful engravings of J. Hoefnagel, *Archetypa Studiaque* (Frankfort 1592). Some of the birds and animals were copied from engravings by A. Collaert, published in Antwerp. Thomas Johnson's business, situated at the Royal Exchange in the City of London, appears to have been acquired by Thomas Jenner. Better known publishers of engravings were Peter Stent, who published from 1643 to 1667 at the sign of the White Horse, Giltspur Street, and John Overton, who published at the White Horse in Little Britain, and the White Horse without Newgate from 1667 to 1707, when he retired and was succeeded by his son. All these addresses under the same sign were so near to each other in the vicinity of St. Bartholomew's Hospital, that Mr. Nevinson concludes they were all the same business.

Like those of Thomas Johnson, the prints published by Peter Stent and John Overton are frank borrowings from other engravings. These plates were copied or bought. The elephant with curving trunk, seen first in Johnson's book, appears finally in Stent's *A Booke of Beasts lively drawne* (B.M. 432.k.1(1)) with a corner of the plate broken off. These direct line-for-line borrowings from other publications result in the marigold, for example, with bud and diagonally slit stem, being printed taller than the elephant which appears on the same page of Johnson's book, and the honeysuckle being depicted larger than the horse, which accounts for the discrepancy in size between the motifs when they were finally transferred directly on to the canvas or satin by the needlewoman or draughtsman.

A key piece to these needlework pictures is a panel of fine tent stitch at Mellerstain, Berwickshire, dated 1706. It was worked by the two daughters of Lady Grisell Baillie, Grisell and Rachel, under the direction of their governess, May Menzies, when they were fourteen and ten years old respectively.

May Menzies had been appointed governess to the girls the previous August, when their mother wrote *Directions for Grisie given May Menzies*:

> To rise by seven a clock and goe about her duty of reading, etc. etc. and be drest and come to Breakfast at nine, to play on the spinet till eleven, from eleven till twelve to write and read French, at two a clock sow her seam till four, at four learn arithmetic, after that dance and play on the spinet again till six and play herself till supper and be in bed at nine.[4]

"To sow her seam" does not, of course, mean plain sewing; at fourteen, Grisie would be past that. Even with the help of May Menzies and Rachel, the fine tent-stitch sampler, still in excellent condition (Plate 21), must have taken the best part of a year to complete, for in 1707, their mother paid for materials and thread "for the bairnses satin piece": another piece of embroidery, perhaps raised work on white satin.

The most remarkable thing about the Mellerstain panel (usually referred to as a sampler) is the fact that with it has been preserved the book, belonging to May Menzies their governess, from which all the motifs on the panel, except the dog and hare, were traced directly on to the canvas. Because the dog and hare are not in the book, and are clumsily drawn, it would seem that this indispensable pair, seldom absent from such pictures, were drawn in by the girls or their governess. The book, which is a volume of Thomas Johnson's *A Booke of Beast . . .*, 1630, was inherited by May Menzies from her grandmother, Katherine Logan, whose initials, K.L. are impressed on the vellum binding. Bound in with the pages of engravings is a set of five sheets showing half-length female figures representing the *Five Senses*, with verses in English beneath. Each figure has an animal attribute: *Hearing*, at the organ, has a picture of deer on the wall. *Sight*, gazing at her reflection in the mirror, has an eagle, renowned for its keen sight, while *Smelling*, chosen as the centrepiece of the panel, has a woman in a flower-crowned hat, with a basket of flowers and nosegay in her hand, with a dog, typifying keen scent (Plate 22).

The book and the panel, which have, happily, been kept together, show how such tent-stitch pictures were created. In this case the motifs were traced directly on to the canvas from the book without any alteration in size. Some are in mirror image. Many of the pages show outlines traced on the reverse side against the light. The flowers were chosen from pictures in the book, not from the garden at Mellerstain, indeed, the olive and vine in the picture cannot have grown in the garden. A symbolic significance is often given to the motifs appearing in these pictures. The pink, for instance, is often regarded as a Stuart emblem. Although it appears on the panel, the Baillie family were anything but Jacobites. Lady Grisell's father, Sir Patrick Hume, had been obliged to escape to Holland during the reign of James II, her husband's father was executed, and her family had lived in exile till they returned with William of Orange in 1688. The peacock has a central position, and might be thought symbolic, until we learn from the accounts that Lady Grisell bought a peacock for Mellerstain in 1704, two years before the sampler was completed (Plate 23).

It is customary to date these pictures by the costume worn by the personages on them. The Mellerstain panel shows how unreliable this can be. The figures depicting the *Five Senses* are wearing the fashions of 1630–40; indeed, *Touch*, an old blind woman whose pet bird pecks her hand, is wearing the ruff of an even earlier date. The panel is, however, of the eighteenth century. If it had not been dated and documented, it could easily have been thought that it was made some seventy or eighty years earlier than its true date.

In this particular case, the motifs were traced directly on to the canvas from the book belonging to the governess, May Menzies. It would be wrong to assume, however, that this was the method adopted in transferring the designs of all such needlework pictures, however similar the motifs. In many of the panels, even those deriving from the same engraving, such as de Jode's *Abraham and the Angels*, the size and accompanying details vary. It may be assumed that the engraving or a group of figures in an engraving, was used as a model by a draughtsman unskilled in figure drawing. But it is unlikely that all these scenes were drawn out by the needlewoman herself, even if she owned the engraving. It would appear that they were often drawn out for her, and though there is as yet no definitive evidence, the canvas or satin for these pictures may have been available to order from printsellers and others.

The widespread use of printed pictures to aid designers was not, of course, confined to the domestic needlewoman, nor was it limited to Britain. The engravings of Bernard Salomon, for instance, were used by embroideresses in Protestant Switzerland[5] and in Catholic Spain.[6] The flowers and birds printed in Johnson's and Stent's books appear on Danish linen embroideries of the seventeenth century.[7] Decorative painters, metal engravers, and sculptors used printed designs; carved stone panels at Edzell Castle were copied from the engravings of Meister I B of Nuremburg. A Spanish painter, Juan Antonio de Frias y Escalante (1630–1670) used a print from a Dutch series engraved by Saenredam after Bloemart, dated 1604, as a model for his painting of the *Expulsion from Paradise*.[8]

A set of four remarkable needlework pictures may be included here. They show conventional subjects: the *Finding of Moses*, *Esther before Ahasuerus, Susanna and the Elders*, and *Jephtha's Daughter*. They hang in St. Nicholas Kirk, Aberdeen, and although they conform in choice of subject to the seventeenth-century small needlework picture, they are more properly wall hangings, for they are all some six feet high, and vary in length from twelve feet, six inches (*Jephtha's Daughter*) to just over seven feet for the other three. They were bought in 1686 "for the decorment of the King's Loft in St. Nicholas Kirk" by the Town Council of Aberdeen, who paid Baillie George Aedie £400 Scots (£33 6s. 8d. sterling) for them. The Moses panel has Aedie's initials G.A.E. and those of his wife, Mary Jamesone, who is believed to have worked them. They could, of course, have been commissioned, but there seems no reason to doubt the tradition that the initials are those of the embroideress. They are by no means professional either in their drawing or execution. Mary Jamesone was the daughter of George Jamesone, the portrait painter, and married George Aedie as her third husband in 1677. She died in 1684.

The panels, worked on linen, with wool, silk and flax threads, are mainly in long and short stitch, with satin, split, stem, Roumanian stitch and French knots. Esther and Pharaoh's daughter show traces of raised and lace stitches on their costume. Esther's brooch and bracelets are of metal thread couched with silk. Scrolled borders, which appear to have been joined on to increase the depth, run along the top and bottom. The borders of the Susanna panel are of a different design, of renaissance fountains and masks. They are laid horizontally, though the pattern is intended to be vertical. There is evidence that more than one hand contributed to the embroidery, as is to be expected in such large pieces.

The colours of the panels are remarkably unfaded, mainly because they have never been exposed to strong sunlight, though they have been moved several times over the centuries when each side of the church (in reality two churches) was rebuilt: one side by James Gibbs in 1755, and the other in 1835 and again in 1875. The panels were mounted as a single group on "strong old canvas fishing sails" and were rescued, wet and smoke-begrimed, after a fire burnt down the steeple and east church in 1874. They were then cleaned and photographed together with a smaller needlework panel of *Jacob wrestling with the Angel*, now lost, which had been used as a table cover on which the church plate was laid at Easter and Christmas. The four large panels were then placed in the vestibule of Gibbs's West Kirk, where they can now be seen, and around 1880 were framed and glazed in order to prevent people from pilfering the threads.

NEEDLEWORK PICTURES

In spite of their large size, and their history as church furnishings, they are essentially domestic pieces, in the tradition of the smaller needlework pictures of their period. The choice of subject and the evident delight in portraying Bible heroines in richly-coloured court costume (except, of course, Susanna), as well as the variety of stitches, are all the mark of a domestic needlewoman. Like the smaller pictures, the designs would appear to follow Bible engravings, and Mrs. Cabot has identified that of Esther as being copied from the engraving taken from the design of Martin van Heemskercke in N. Visscher's *Historiae Sacrae Veteris et Novi Testamenti* published in Amsterdam around 1660 (Plates 24 and 25). Unlike the Mellerstain panel, the design could not be traced directly on to the linen, and a draughtsman of some skill would be required to transfer so faithfully the lines of the engraving, 40 cm. high by 50 cm. wide, on to a linen panel 152 cm. by 213 cm. (5 feet by 7 feet). On account of their large size, Dr. W. Kelly, who pieced together the history of these panels,[9] assumed that they had been worked by Mary Jamesone as a young woman, in her father's studio after his death in 1644. The Esther panel cannot have been made so early and it would appear more likely that the Moses panel was made after her marriage to George Aedie in 1677. The size of the panels would not have prevented her working on them after she married. It will be seen in the next chapter that large hangings requiring frames continued to be made in domestic surroundings up to the beginning of the nineteenth century, with the help of the family and household, and indeed large quilting frames are known to have been accommodated in Welsh and Durham cottages until the present day.

REFERENCES

1. NEVINSON, J. L., "Peter Stent and John Overton, publishers of embroidery designs," *Apollo*, XXIV, Nov. 1936, pp. 279–83.
Also *English Domestic Embroidery Patterns of the sixteenth and seventeenth centuries*, Walpole Society, Vol. XXVIII, 1940.

Also *Catalogue of English Domestic Embroidery*, Victoria and Albert Museum 1938, p. xxv.

2. CABOT, N. G., "Pattern sources of scriptural subjects in Tudor and Stuart embroideries," *Bulletin of the Needle and Bobbin Club*, New York, Vol. 30, No. 1, 1946, pp. 3–54.

3. UNTERMYER, I., *English and other Needlework*, Thames and Hudson. London, 1960, Figs. 51 and 66. Detail of Fig. 175.

4. *The Household Book of Lady Grisell Baillie 1692–1733*. The Scottish History Society, 1911, p. xlvii. I am indebted to the Earl of Haddington, K.T., for allowing me to study the panel and book at Mellerstain.

5. TRUDEL, V., *Schweizerische Leinenstickereien*, Bern, 1954, pl. xv.

6. *A devotional miscellany*, Museum of Fine Arts, Boston, 1966. Tobias, See CABOT, N. G., op. cit., p. 17.

7. GARDE, G., *Danske silkebroderede laerredsduge fra 16 og 17 arhundrede med saerligt henblick pa de grafiske forbilleder*, København, 1961.

8. Shown in the exhibition of Spanish Painting, Bowes Museum, Barnard Castle, 1967. Cat. no. 57.

9. KELLY, W., "Four needlework pictures attributed to Mary Jamesone," *Miscellany of the Third Spalding Club*, Vol. II, Aberdeen, 1941.

Plate 24. Panel from St. Nicholas Kirk, Aberdeen, attributed to Mary Jamesone. Esther before Ahasuerus. The panel, with four others, was bought by Aberdeen Town Council in 1686 from George Aedie, husband of Mary Jamesone, who had died in 1684, 'for the decorment of the King's Loft in St. Nicholas Kirk', and has remained in the church since.

Coloured wools and silk on linen.

Long and short stitch, satin, split, stem, Roumanian stitch and French knots, raised and lace stitch. Esther's brooch and bracelets are of metal thread couched with silk. The border at the top and foot, worked on twill, has been added to give depth.   152 × 213 cm.

The Kirk Session of St. Nicholas Kirk, Aberdeen

PECTORE SOLLICITO SED NON TRISTI OMINE REGEM CONVENIENS ESTER, FERCULA AD ALMA VOCAT. Esther Cap 5 v 1

Plate 25. Engraving. Esther before Ahasuerus, from *Historia Sacrae Veteris et Novi Testamenti*, drawn by Martin van Heemskercke published by N. Visscher, Amsterdam c. 1660.   40 × 50 cm.   C 157.b.25.

British Museum

Plate 26. Two panels of a six fold screen signed and dated JULIA CALVERLEY 1727. She was the wife of Sir Walter Calverley, who is reputed to have been the model of Addison's Sir Roger de Coverley. The left panel shows at the top bees swarming, and below, basket weaving and the making of agricultural implements. These are taken from the illustrations to the works of Virgil, drawn by Francis Cleyn, published first in Paris in 1641. An English translation was published in London by John Ogilby in 1654.

Coloured wools and silk on canvas. Each panel about 176·5 × 53 cm.

The National Trust, Wallington Hall, Northumberland

Plate 27. Engraving. *The Swarming of bees* from Book IV of Virgil's Georgics. From the design by Francis Cleyn, engraved by W. Hollar. P. VIRGILII MARONIS *Opera* Paris 1641. 26·5 × 19 cm.

The University Library, Edinburgh

Plate 28. Engraving. *The making of agricultural implements* from Book II of Virgil's Georgics. From the design by Francis Cleyn, engraved by W. Hollar. P. VIRGILII MARONIS *Opera* Paris 1641.   *The University Library, Edinburgh*

Plate 29. Wall hanging signed and dated Anne Grant 1750. An arcaded terrace with vases of flowers and a tree standing on black and white tiles against a yellow background. Wool and silk on canvas.
Fine tent stitch.   182·9 × 240 cm.   *Lady Jean Grant of Monymusk*

7

Wall Hangings

A letter to the *Spectator* of October 13th, 1714, states:

I have a couple of nieces under my direction who so often run giddy abroad that I don't know where to have them. Their dress, their tea, and their visits take up all their time, and they go to bed as tired with doing nothing as I am after quilting a whole under-petticoat. The only time they are not idle is while they read your *Spectator*; which being dedicated to the interests of virtue, I desire you to recommend the long-neglected art of needlework. Those hours which in this age are thrown away in dress, play, visits and the like, were employed in my time in writing out receipts, or working beds, chairs and hangings for the family. For my part, I have plied my needle these fifty years, and would never have it out of my hand. It grieves my heart to see a couple of proud idle flirts sipping their tea, for a whole afternoon, in a room hung with the industry of their great-grandmother. . . .

With gentle irony 'Mr Spectator' replied:

In obedience to the commands of my venerable correspondent I have duly weighed this important subject, and promise myself, from all the arguments here laid down, all the fine ladies of England will be ready, as soon as their mourning is over [public mourning for Queen Anne, who died August 1st, 1714] to appear covered in the work of their own hands.

What a delightful entertainment it must be for the fair sex, whom their native modesty, and the tenderness of men towards them, exempts from public business, to pass their hours in imitating fruit and flowers, and transplanting all the beauties of nature into their own dress, or raising a new creation in their closets and apartments. How pleasing is the amusement of walking the shades and groves planted by themselves, in surveying heroes slain by their needle. . . .

In an exceedingly pert reply, published on October 20th, 1714, 'Cleora' rejected his suggestion that ladies should fill their time with needlework:

> . . . I love birds and beasts as well as you, but am content to fancy them when they are ready made. What do you think of gilt leather for furniture? There's your pretty hanging for a chamber, and what is more, our own country is the only place in Europe where work of that kind is tolerably done. Without minding your musty lessons, I am this morning going to St. Paul's Churchyard to bespeak a screen and a set of hangings, and am resolved to encourage the manufacture of my country.

In spite of this amusing exchange in the *Spectator* the fashion for embroidered hangings did not go out at the beginning of the eighteenth century, and there were still ladies outside London who embarked on the daunting enterprise of providing sets of several large wall hangings to decorate their own homes. Woven tapestries were commissioned by those who could afford the cost from France or other continental countries, or as 'Cleora's' ambiguous reply might suggest, needlework hangings could be made to order around St. Paul's in London, close to the printsellers' shops in Newgate and Little Britain. But there were still others who enjoyed needlework for its own sake and felt capable of making their own.

Very few of these large hangings have survived. Many have perished, destroyed by moth and dust; some have been cut up to make bed hangings, bedcovers or screens. But the chief cause of their disappearance was the introduction of painted and later, in the second half of the eighteenth century, of printed wallpaper. It provided a light and charming decoration for walls in place of the dark and dusty hangings, so difficult to clean. Most of the wall hangings were understandably swept away when a house was renovated or rebuilt; those that have survived have done so almost by accident. Six late seventeenth-century panels in wool on canvas now in the Victoria and Albert Museum (517 to 522–1896) were found behind plaster in a house in Hatton Garden, London. The set of four large hangings worked by Mary Jamesone in Aberdeen escaped destruction because they were all scriptural subjects from the Old Testament, and therefore considered suitable for a Presbyterian church. It has been conjectured that they were made for the walls of an oblong room in George Aedie's house, which was demolished in 1914, with the smaller lost panel of *Jacob wrestling with the Angel*, hanging over the chimneypiece.[1]

Perhaps the best documented set of wall hangings are those worked by Lady Julia Calverley, at Wallington, Northumberland.[2] The ten hangings, each 290 cm. deep by 90 cm. wide (9 feet 6 inches by 35 inches), are worked on canvas in tent stitch in wool and silk on a white ground, said to be worked in cotton. They are enclosed in narrow carved frames attached to the walls. One is inscribed *1717 Julia Calverley*. On February 27th, 1716, Sir Walter Calverley had noted in his Memorandum Book: "My wife finished the sewed work in the drawing room, having been three years and a half in the doing. The greatest part has been done with her own hands. It consists of ten panels." Even with the help of her family and maids to work the background, for instance, it shows great diligence and determination to have finished the panels in so short a time. Tent stitch is, however, well adapted for a communal effort of this kind: three needlewomen of varying competence can produce a completely harmonious result, as the Mellerstain panel demonstrates.

The designs of Lady Julia Calverley's hangings are extremely well drawn, and show flowing branches arising from hillocks all richly covered with exotic blooms and birds. Mr. Wingfield Digby suggests that the designs were selected in London, which Sir Walter is known to have visited regularly. A six-fold screen inscribed *Julia Calverley 1727* is also worked in tent stitch on canvas in wool and silk (Plates 26, 27 and 28). It shows scenes of country pursuits, five of them taken, with some slight modifications, from

51

Virgil's *Eclogues and Georgics*, published by John Ogilby in London in 1654, and illustrated by Francis Cleyn, who had been brought to this country in 1623 under the patronage of Charles I (then Prince of Wales) and appointed designer to the Mortlake tapestry manufactory.

A design from the same source – this time Cleyn's illustration to Virgil's *Aeneid* published by Ogilby in 1658, appears on another remarkable set of wall hangings. This is the set from Stoke Edith, Herefordshire, a house destroyed by fire in 1947. The hangings are now at Montacute House, Somerset. The design, which shows Aeneas and Achates confronted by Venus in the guise of a huntress before Carthage, conforms much more closely to Cleyn's engraving than do Lady Julia Calverley's five screen panels. Two other large oblong panels from Stoke Edith show in vivid detail with sharply cast shadows, sections of a formal garden in springtime, one with a group at table in the open air wearing costumes of the first decade of the eighteenth century. The panels have been ascribed to the five successive wives of the second Thomas Foley of Stoke Edith who succeeded to the estate in 1737 and married his last wife in 1744. This tradition is disputed[3] because the panels are not mentioned in Thomas Foley's detailed accounts, and furthermore, one shows the crest of Knightley of Fawsley, which was that of the wife of the first Thomas Foley who died in 1737. They were not recorded by the observant Celia Fiennes on her third visit to Stoke Edith, some time after 1699. They may, indeed, have been, like 'Cleora's' in the *Spectator*, bespoken from St. Paul's Churchyard some time between 1700 and 1737. The garden scenes especially, which originally adorned the Green Velvet bedroom at Stoke Edith, are a delightfully sunny decoration for any room.

An equally bright hanging, due mainly to its yellow background, is one at Monymusk, Aberdeenshire, signed *Anne Grant 1750* (Plate 29). It is worked in fine tent stitch in wool and silk and measures 240 cm. in width by 203 cm. high (7 feet 10½ inches by 6 feet 8 inches). Vases of flowers and a potted tree stand on black and white tiles against a golden yellow background, under three arches supported by flower-wreathed columns. Anne Grant was the sister of the agricultural reformer, Sir Francis Grant of Monymusk.

WALL HANGINGS

Another set of hangings is at Aston Hall, Birmingham, together with an embroidered carpet. One of the hangings bears the inscription:

God be the Guide
And the work will abide
Mary Holte Spinster Aged LX
Anno Dom. MDCXLIV

One of the hangings shows a view of Aston Hall, another shows Brereton Hall, which also belonged to the Holte family.

Large hangings in tent stitch, although extremely durable, are very slow to complete, and Lady Julia Calverley's ten panels in three and a half years, even with extra help, must be considered something of a record. A more rapid method of making hangings is to embroider in worsted on to a firmly woven background. This was the method used for crewel work bed curtains on a twill background. Some of the large pieces, now serving as bedcovers, may well have been wall hangings originally, cut down for their present use. A large wall hanging, now in the National Museum of Scottish Antiquities, came from the Hirsel, Berwickshire, and shows the arms of Alexander Home and Janet Drummond, his second wife, and was worked about 1740. It has a deep scrolled border with thistles. Below the coat of arms with the motto *True to the End*, is a vase of flowers. This exceptionally large hanging – it measures 518 cm. deep by 273 cm. wide (17 feet by 9 feet) – is embroidered in coloured wools in long and short stitch, laid work and a tied stitch, and worked on an unusual material, a plain weave of tightly twisted worsted. It was large and warm, but much more quickly worked than a tent-stitch hanging.

Another method utilizing a firmly woven background was, of course, to apply smaller embroidered motifs. This was the technique used in late medieval church embroidery when gold work was applied to vestments and altar hangings of velvet, damask or satin. In the inventory of goods belonging to Dame Alice Hungerford, attainted for murder in 1524, there was "a hanging of red say with a hundert peyre of pyn apples imbrodered with golde to put on the said hanging".[4] It was the method used by the

53

embroiderers of Mary Queen of Scots and the Countess of Shrewsbury, when cloth of gold, sometimes from vestments, was applied
with velvet and silk to other backgrounds to make large hangings
for walls and beds. Indeed, most Scottish inventories distinguish
between tent stitch and applied embroidery by using the word
sewed for tent stitch (as did Sir Walter Calverley), and *broderit* or
brouderit for appliqué work. The Lochleven and Linlithgow hangings have a mixture of yellow silk embroidery and applied velvet
on the red woollen background. Most of the beds belonging to
Mary Queen of Scots appear to have been decorated with this
mixture of embroidery and cloth appliqué.

Fine tent-stitch motifs could also be applied economically to wall
hangings. The uncut panels at Traquair (see Plate 8) were probably intended for walls or beds. Slips of plants, birds, and animals
in fine tent stitch are applied to wall panels of eighteenth-century
cream silk damask at Lennoxlove, the house bought by the Trustees
of the will of Frances Stuart ("La belle Stuart"), Duchess of Richmond and Lennox (1647–1702). Originally several rooms were
embellished with these motifs; only one now retains this form of
decoration.

Perhaps the most remarkable appliqué wall hangings were the
set of fourteen, designed by the architect, Robert Adam, for the
drawing-room at Newliston, West Lothian. His father, William
Adam, had designed a mansion at Newliston for Field-Marshal the
2nd Earl of Stair, which, though illustrated in *Vitruvius Scoticus*,
1810, was never built. The estate was bought by Roger Hog, whose
son, Thomas Hog commissioned Robert Adam in 1789 to draw up
revised plans for Newliston. Robert Adam died in 1792 before
the house was quite finished. The panels were all apparently worked
by Lady Mary Maitland, wife of Thomas Hog. They were married
in 1773, and she died in 1795.

In 1845 new wings were added to the house by the architect,
David Bryce, when a wall with two of the panels on it was
demolished. These two panels still remain at Newliston in good
condition, as they had been stored away, but the remaining twelve
deteriorated beyond repair, and were sold at Sotheby's in 1928,
their present whereabouts are unknown.[5] The largest measured

236 cm. high by 251 cm. wide (7 feet 9 inches by 8 feet 3 inches). Five others were of the same height, but of varying widths to fit the panels round the room; the other six were smaller. They showed urns of flowers supported by sphinxes, with small medallions of figures, such as the nine Muses, wearing classical drapery. The two panels that remain show a framed oval medallion of silver grey, presumably representing a mirror, hanging over a cornice supporting two smoking vases. A basket of flowers hangs from the cornice, containing auriculas and moss roses (Plate 30).

Although no signed drawings for the panels remain, the design of the whole set was sufficiently distinctive to be accepted as Robert Adam's work, or at least as drawn by one of his assistants at the time the house was designed. He was accustomed to designing the interior decoration of his buildings, of course, such as the stucco work, furniture and even carpets, but there appears to be no record of his using embroidered wall panels in any other house he designed. Panels embroidered in silk were, however, used by Micque and Rousseau de la Rottière, the French architects, to decorate the walls of the boudoir of Marie Antoinette at Fontainebleau, built in 1785.

The panels at Newliston are unusual, not because of their designer, but because of their technique. They are worked on a cream woollen repp, which was called *moreen* in the eighteenth century, and the design is built up by applying pieces of felt, cut to the desired shapes, and tinted apparently with water colour, to the background, and then holding them down with widely spaced stitches in silk thread. As well as being extremely effective as a delicately coloured wall decoration, the technique was much more rapid than it would appear, since the felt shapes could be cut out from templates in advance by several helpers. Many of the shapes are repeated several times. They could be tinted, and the whole design rapidly assembled and stitched down on the moreen background stretched flat on a frame. The method would appear to have been suggested by Lady Mary Hog herself, since a bed, complete with curtains, bedcover, back, tester, upper and lower valances, as well as window curtains, still remains at Newliston, ascribed to her, and all decorated with tinted applied felt. The material is moreen of the same quality as the wall panels. It may be the bed for which Thomas Hog, in September 1773, the year of their marriage, paid a bill to Young and Trotter, Upholsterers, Edinburgh. The account included:

A four posted oak bed frame with plain mahogney foot, posts, covered castors double screws canvas bottoms	£5.	5.	0.
65½ yards Superfine yellow moreen 2/4	7.	12.	0.
9 doz 2 yards silk bed lace 3/6	1.	12.	1.
. . . Makeing a four posted Bed furniture of yellow moreen		13.	6.
. . . Makeing 2 window curtains to draw up		5.	0.[6]

Lady Mary Hog did not, of course, invent the technique of felt appliqué. Many charming flower pieces of the period survive, in which the moss rose and the auricula are prominent, the petals tinted and often curled to give a three-dimensional effect, and framed in a deep frame to accommodate the blooms in relief. They are, indeed, eighteenth-century versions of the seventeenth-century raised work picture, executed with greater realism, and are the ancestors of the modern fabric collage (Plate 31).

REFERENCES

1. KELLY, W., "Four Needlework Pictures attributed to Mary Jamesone," *Miscellany of the Third Spalding Club*, Vol. II, Aberdeen, 1941, p. 10.

2. WINGFIELD DIGBY, G., "Lady Julia Calverley, Embroideress," *Connoisseur*, Vol. CXLV, 1960, pp. 82 and 169.

3. JOURDAIN, M., "Needlework Wall Hangings from Stoke Edith," *Country Life Annual*, 1951, pp. 81–88.

4. *Archeologia*, Vol XXXVIII (1860), p. 363, quoted by J. L. Nevinson in *Catalogue of English Domestic Embroidery*, 1938.

5. I am indebted to Major R. T. Hog of Newliston for information about the bed and panels and permission to reproduce the bill.

8

Raised Work

Raised and padded embroidery on satin, which was given the name *stump work* in the nineteenth century,[1] is often regarded as a peculiarly English eccentricity of the seventeenth century. The tiny, doll-like figures, wearing lace-stitch garments of the time of Charles I or II, with wired silk-embroidered flowers often as large as the figures, with birds and crouching beasts and fishponds all attached to white satin and embellished with beads and spangles are familiar and are liable to arouse either delight or derision.

The pictures, mirror frames, and small cabinets show the same figures, flowers and creatures as the tent-stitch pictures of the same period. Indeed, they derive from the same engravings and show the Five Senses, the Four Continents, Kings and Queens and scenes from the Old Testament, all set about with birds and flowers, butterflies and caterpillars, crammed in with the same disregard of scale that is found in the Mellerstain panel. Bible scenes were often taken from engravings by Gerard de Jode (1521–1591) or Jost Amman (1539–1591) whose illustrated books of the Old Testament must have been enormously popular, judging by the number of embroidered pictures copied from them. The 1662 trade list of Peter Stent, who printed and sold engravings in London, shows the range of subjects available in single sheets or books:

A Book of Flora, 13 plates
A book of Flowers, Beafts, Birds and Fruits in
  three parts, 20 leaves in each Part.
A new Book of Flowers, Beafts, Birds, invented
  and drawn wholly by J. Dunftall
A book of Branches, Slips, Flies, etc. 8 Plats

Books in Half-Sheets
The four Seafons of the Year. W. Hollar fecit.
The four Seafons of the Year. G. Glover Sculpt.
The five Senfes, Marmion Inventer.
The five Senfes, Glover Sculpt.
The four Quarters of the World.
The four Complexions, in habit of 4 Nations.
The four Elements, Fire, Aire, Earth and Water . . .
Fiolet's Drawing Book, being useful for to teach to Draw,
  Etch, Paint &c. 10 Plats.

Pictures lately Printed in Sheets
Queen Elizabeth.
King James and Queen Anne.
King Charles the First and Queen Mary.
King Charles the Second and Queen Katharine.
Two other sorts of the King.
Duke of York.
Duke of Gloucester.
Prince of Orange and Princefs Royal . . .

Over 500 titles are listed on the trade sheet which ends: "Thefe, with many other forts of Prints, Maps, and Copy Books, are Printed and Sold by Peter Stent, at the Sign of the White-Horfe in Gilt-Fpur Ftreet, without Newgate 1662."[2]

The kings and queens of the needlework pictures are seldom identifiable; indeed, it could be that the costume from a print of Queen Henrietta Maria might have been used as a model for Queen Esther's courtly garments as she kneels before Ahasuerus, but a curious strip in raised embroidery on silk at Jedburgh shows a mounted King labelled K I, and a queen with the initials Q A, which would appear to identify the figures as James I and Anne of Denmark (Plate 32).

Engravings were equally useful for pictures in tent stitch or raised work, drawn on to canvas or thick white satin. Raised work pictures can often be found with part of the design uncovered, finely drawn out in ink. Firm padding, carved boxwood heads and arms, detached needlepoint curtains and garments, pearls, spangles and metal thread, all combine to give a three-dimensional effect, though there is little attempt at perspective, and the architecture in the background appears generally to have been copied from the earliest printed Bibles, such as the Cologne Bible of Heinrich Quentel (1479).

Embroidery in high relief developed much later in Britain than in other European countries. By the end of the fifteenth century, in Germany and its neighbours, Austria, Hungary, Bohemia and Moravia, ecclesiastical embroidery had become much more three-dimensional, emulating wood carving. A violet satin chasuble in Brno, Czechoslovakia (Plate 33) dated 1487, shows the Virgin with the saint known to us as Good King Wenceslas, highly modelled with gaunt cheekbones and curling dark hair and beard, wearing armour and a curving cloak of laid metal thread, his right hand supporting a shield, his left, which perhaps once held a banner, raised and free. In Munich two wings of a south German reliquary of 1519 bear the figures in relief of Saint Sebastian and Saint Ursula, applied to white satin. Their faces are modelled and their robes are thick with seed pearls.[3] Other church embroideries in high relief of this period are to be found in Spain, Poland and Sweden. Perhaps the most remarkable is a diptych[4] of the early sixteenth century from Hungary, showing the suffering heads of Christ and the Virgin modelled with a painful naturalism. It shows the final flowering of Gothic realism which was replaced in the seventeenth century by a Baroque splendour, especially in Flanders. Highly modelled fruit, covered with laid silks of brilliant colours, spill from golden cornucopiae on altar frontals; a set of altar-pieces, designed by Rubens in this baroque style, survives in Belgium.

The Reformation prevented Britain from following this continental trend. Unlike the Calvinist Church of Scotland, the Church of England did not banish embroidery. Altar linen, such as chalice veils, continued to be decorated with needlework, though it was not until the middle of the seventeenth century that even the Anglican church could adopt without embarrassment embroidered representations of Christ and the Saints, and then only under High Church influence. An altar cushion at Winchester College made in

1636 or 1637 shows the *Last Supper* with the Four Evangelists in the corners, and is worked in high relief. The same scene also decorates an altar-dossal of 1633 in private ownership,[5] which is thought to have come from the workshop of Edmund Harrison, who held the office of Royal Embroiderer in London under Charles I.

In Scotland, professional embroiderers were working in Edinburgh throughout the seventeenth century to produce heraldic work, though with the court removed to London, except for brief visits, they must have been hard put to it to find sufficient work to keep the craft alive. Several were made Burgesses: Johne Betoun, brodinster 1608, perhaps a son of William Beatoun *broudister to the Kingis Majesty as merchant*, who had been made Burgess and gild-brother on April 29th, 1597 "by the Kingis majesties speciall wryting direct to the provest baillies and councell to that effect". There were also James White (Quhyte), browdster, (1613), William White, his eldest son (1620), and James White, another son (1631). In 1638 two embroiderers, Alexander Barnes and Hew Tod were working in the Canongate.

Raised and padded embroidery was particularly suitable for heraldic hangings and two survive from the seventeenth century in Edinburgh. One showing the arms of James I and VI with a favourite motto of his, *BEATI SUNT PACIFICI*, may have been made for the occasion of the monarch's visit to Edinburgh in 1617. The other shows the arms of Charles II and may be those referred to in the Burgh Records of Edinburgh for 1661 where the City Council "appoynts the Theasaurer . . . to agrie with Robert Porteus for imbrothering the King's Majesties armes as formerlie to be put up in the Session hous . . ." after Charles had ordered the City Council to prepare the Inner Parliament House "in that forme and fashioun as it wont to be when the Lords of his Majesties Counsell and Session or the Committee of Estates did sitt there".

On the other hand, it may have been ordered from London, for a letter is recorded from Lords Lauderdale and Bellenden, headed: "Whitehall, March 17th, 1668". It begins: "Right Honourable— Wee have received the Note of such things as are to be provided for the Councill and Session house; And in order to the providing of them Wee went in to London yesterday." Descriptions and prices of tapestries, table carpets, chairs, clocks, candlesticks and a mace are followed by "The peece of Hanging with the King's Armes, for the Session house will be longest a doing, but it shall be bespoke."[6]

Even after this date, the few remaining pieces of professional embroidery from Edinburgh workshops show a surprisingly high standard of workmanship in spite of restricted demand. The thistles and large shoulder badge showing St. Andrew on the robes of the eight Knights of the Thistle, re-instituted by James II and VII in 1687 are competently worked (Plate 34). The badge on the Archer's bonnet of pale blue velvet ornamented with silver lace, ordered by James, 4th Earl of Wemyss in 1726, when he was appointed Lieutenant-General of the Company of Archers, also shows St. Andrew, worked in silver thread and silks. The bill for the bonnet survives: [7]

JAMES CUMING

To 1 blew Velvet Bonnett	£0. 14. 0
To 1 embroidered St. Andrew	0. 7. 6
To 2¼ yds silver and green ribbon at 2/2	4. 10½
To 1¼ yds Richest Open silver lace at 12/-	15. 0
To 9½ Drop silver fringe at 9/–	0. 5. 4
	£2. 6. 8½

It may have been a sign of the times that as the number of professional male embroiderers declined in Edinburgh, embroidery was specified as being taught in girls' schools. The Edinburgh Council Minute, June 25th, 1662 "Gives warrand and libertie to Mistress Christian Cleland to keip a schole within the burgh of Edinburgh, Canongait, Leith, West Port, Potterrow or any place within the bounds and jurisdiction of Edinburgh for teaching and instructing of all scholleris who sall come to her and that ather in reading, wrytting, singing, playing, danceing, speaking of the

Frensh tongue, arithmetic, shewing, embroidering, or any uther thign quhilk the said Christian is able to teache and for that effect to provide herself with dancing masteris, singing masteris, playing masteris, Frensh masteris and all utheris persones quherof she stands in neid for the education of her said schollers . . ."

It is not known what types of embroidery were taught by Mrs. Cleland, but it is highly probable that raised work on white satin was among them, for in 1700 another Edinburgh schoolmistress, Elizabeth Straiton, sent an account to the Laird of Kilravock, for his daughter Margaret's education : [8]

Accompt the Laird of Kilraith for his daughter, Mrs. (sic) Margaret Rose for her board and education, to Elizabeth Stratoun 1700 Imprimis, one quarter board, from the 2nd September to the 2nd December £60. 0. 0.

Item, Dancing, one quarter	14. 10.	0.

Item One quarter singing and Playing, and virginalls.

Shee having two Masters for playing, I payed a dollar more to the second then the first	11. 12.	0.
Item One quarter at wryting	6. 0.	0.
Item For five writting books	1. 0.	0.
Item Fat (?For) Satine seame and silk to her satine seame	6. 0.	0.
Item One sett of wax-fruits	6. 0.	0.
Item One looking glass that she broke	4. 16.	0.
Item A frame for a satine seam	1. 10.	0.
. . . Item a glass for her satine seam	1. 4.	0.

The item for the broken looking-glass makes one suspect that the 'satin seam' was originally intended as a mirror frame many of which were decorated with raised work. The wax fruits may have been used as moulds, covered with silks, or else they may have replaced the broken mirror as centrepiece. At any rate, it was finished and glazed and framed, and no doubt taken by Margaret to her new home when she married the following year.

Lady Grisell Baillie's two daughters also undertook an embroidery on satin, in 1707, the year after they finished the tent-stitch picture under the direction of their governess, May Menzies. Lady Grisell notes in her accounts:

Edinburgh 1707.

May. To ¼ whit satin for the bairenses satin pece	£1.	2.	6.
For silks to it 6s. nails, threed to the tent 1s.		7.	0.
For silk to make a purs and strings 13s		13.	0.

(Scots)

A quarter of an ell suggests a small picture, not a mirror frame or a casket, but no piece survives which can be identified. No doubt the book of engravings belonging to their governess which was used for the tent-stich panel, would be used again to provide the motifs for the 'satin pece'. The well-known birds and flowers, the flies and caterpillars, were all at hand for a traditional raised work picture. The flowers worked in detached needlepoint stitches of silk stiffened with wire, or that form the little 'garden' when the lid of the casket is opened, were certainly traditional, for they were amongst the articles left behind by Mary Queen of Scots: "One uther coffer wrocht of cantailyie (tassels) of gold with medallis of moder of perll contenand lxxviii flouris maid of wyre coverit with silk of divers cullouris and a porcupenis pen."

The caskets or cabinets, made of white satin, usually with a sloping top and smaller lid, have doors at the front to reveal drawers, often covered in silk laid work in a geometrical pattern. The top, sides, front and back are embroidered in raised work motifs.

So frequently do the motifs recur on these pictures, mirror frames, and caskets, that it is thought that the designs could be bought ready drawn on to the satin, though no proof is yet available. Certainly many of the cabinets are made up to a stock pattern: even the 'secret' drawers are in the same place. It would appear that once the needlewoman had completed the top, sides and drawer fronts, the work was returned to the shop from which the designs were bought, to be made up to a stock pattern, often lined with pink silk. This theory is strengthened by a letter found in the casket of Hannah Smith, now in the Whitworth Art Gallery,

Manchester. Because of this letter, the casket may be regarded as much a key piece for these embroidered cabinets as the Mellerstain panel is for the tent-stitch pictures. The casket, in coloured silks, gilt and silver thread and spangles on white satin, has comparatively little raised work: only a single figure on the lid (Plates 35 and 36), which shows Joseph being raised from the pit and sold to the Midianite merchants by his brothers. The figures of Joseph and his two brothers lifting him up are taken from the scene in G. de Jode's *Thesaurus* 1585 (Plate 37). The familiar lion and leopard on either side of the top lock scroll are also in raised work. The front door-panels are worked in fine tent and rococo stitch with seed pearls, and show Deborah and Barak, and Jael and Sisera. On the sides below the handles are Autumn (Ceres) and Winter, a man with a cat before a fire.

Its value as a key piece rests upon the enchanting letter written by Hannah Smith:

> The year of Our Lord being 1657.
> if ever I have any thoughts about the time; when I went to Oxford: as it may be I may: when I have forgotten the time, to fortifi my self: I may look in this paper and find it: I went to Oxford; in the year of 1654; as my being there near 2 years. for I went in 1654; and stayed there in 1655, and I came away in 1656, and I was almost 12 years of age; when I went I made an end of my cabbinette, at Oxford and my – . – ? and my cabbinet, was made up, in the year of 1656 at London; I have written this to fortiffi my self, and those that shall inquire about it.
>
> Hannah Smith.

Hannah's casket would also appear to be one of the earliest dated pieces of English raised work. A picture of Esther and Ahasuerus, in the same technique, with the date 1654, the year Hannah went to Oxford, is recorded.[9] It shows the arms of the Dyers Company of London. A casket signed by Martha Edlin, (born 1660) and dated 1671, is additional evidence that these caskets were usually schoolgirls' pieces. In 1668 Martha Edlin had made a sampler in coloured silks with alphabets, followed by a white cutwork

Plate 30. Wall panel of cut and applied felt on corded and watered yellow woollen material, (moreen). A framed mirror on a cornice with a basket of flowers suspended. One of a pair, from a set designed by Robert Adam for Newliston, Midlothian.

Cut and tinted felt shapes, held down by silk couching stitches. About 1793. 134·6 × 106·7 cm.

Major R.T. Hog of Newliston

Plate 31. Felt picture (felt collage) worked in 1790 by Elizabeth Catherine Yorke. A basket of flowers and fruit: auriculas, moss roses, passion flower and cherries. Cut coloured felt applied with silk stitches. 43 × 48 cm.

Lady Victoria Wemyss

Plate 32. Detail of a panel made from three fragments. A mounted horseman with page, with the initials K I for King James I. The figure of a queen appears on the panel with the initials Q A, for his queen, Anne of Denmark. Coloured silks and metal thread on pale green silk, applied silks sometimes padded. Early 17th century.

Long and short, satin, Roumanian stitch and couched metal thread. Bought in 1937 from the collection of William Sanders Fiske for Jedburgh Town House.

Jedburgh Town Council

Plate 33. Figure in high relief on a violet satin chasuble dated 1487. St. Wenceslas. Moravian.

Gold and silk embroidery, heavily padded. The armour is gold, the cloak gold and green, the crown lined with red. Figure 39 cm. high.

Moravska Galerie, Brno, Czeckoslavakia

Plate 34. Mantle of the Order of the Thistle, worn by James, 4th Earl of Perth when the Order was revived by James II in May 1687. The eight knights created on that day all became Jacobites, and the Earl of Perth followed his master into exile. Queen Anne reconstituted the Order in 1703, when a plain green velvet mantle with shoulder badge was ordained.

Gold thistles powdered on green velvet, with an embroidered silver shoulder badge of St. Andrew.

From a private collection

sampler in 1669. In 1671 she presumably finished her casket, and in 1673 completed a jewel case with beadwork, rococo and tent stitches, now in the Victoria and Albert Museum (T.41–1954).

If these raised work caskets, mirror frames and pictures are indeed schoolgirls' pieces, it would explain why trial designs are so seldom found for this type of embroidery on samplers of the period. The satin pieces were themselves samplers. It is true that some of the whitework samplers show figures with some detached needlepoint details (e.g. Victoria and Albert Museum T.6–1910 given by H.M. Queen Mary). However, a sampler signed Mary Lawley 1667, has, in the middle of conventional bands of silk embroidery on linen, a female figure in raised work, the face merely suggested by a circle of padding, but wearing a gown of detached buttonhole stitches in pink and cream, with a deep blue stole over one shoulder (Plate 38).

It has been shown that this type of embroidery continued to be taught in Scotland during the first decade of the eighteenh century. A picture of Esther and Ahasuerus, in the Victoria and Albert Museum, suggests that this was true of Yorkshire also. The picture (892–1864) has an inscription on the back of the frame "This frame made by Robert Addam house carpenter in Selby for Mr. John Blyth Apother in Selby ye 20th day of January anno dom. 1707". It was no doubt worked by the Apothecary's daughter and would have made an admired decoration to a room.

REFERENCES

1. NEVINSON, J. L., *Catalogue of English Domestic Embroidery*, Victoria and Albert Museum, 1938, p. xxi.

2. Bodleian Library, *Gough Maps* 46, p. 160.
See also NEVINSON, J. L., "Peter Stent and John Overton," *Apollo*, Vol. XXIV, no. 145, Nov. 1936, p. 279.

3. SCHUETTE, M. and MÜLLER-CHRISTENSEN, S., *Das Stickereiwerk*, Tübingen, 1963, Pls. 314/315.

4. Exhibition of Hungarian Art, 1967 (Victoria and Albert Museum), Cat. no. 206.

5. WARDLE, P., "A Laudian Embroidery," *Victoria and Albert Museum Bulletin*, Vol. 1, No. 1, Jan. 1965, p. 26.

6. HENSHALL, A., and MAXWELL, S., "Two seventeenth century embroidered Royal Coats of Arms," Proc. of the Soc. of Antiquaries of Scotland Vol. XCV, 1961–2, p. 284. I am grateful for the authors' permission to quote from this work.

7. Quoted by permission of Captain Michael Wemyss.

8. *The Family of Rose of Kilravock*, Spalding Club, Aberdeen, 1848, p. 388.

9. NEVINSON, J. L., *Catalogue of English Domestic Embroidery*, Victoria and Albert Museum, 1938 p. 41.

9

Chair Seats and a Carpet

Needlework wall hangings and bed curtains afforded warmth, embroidered pictures added decoration, but there were still other ways of adding comfort and colour to the home. Until the second half of the seventeenth century, loose cushions were more common than covered chairs, for they could be used on wooden benches. In 1565 at Holyroodhouse two cushions of cramoisie velvet stuffed with feathers were issued "to serve in the chapel". Loose cushions had the additional advantage that they could be easily packed when moving from place to place, as, for instance, when the court moved from Edinburgh to Stirling or Linlithgow.

In the royal Inventory of 1578, ten years after Mary had left Scotland, there were ten chairs listed in Edinburgh Castle, nine velvet covered and one covered with leather, also fourteen folding stools (two "coverit with sewit werk of divers culloris")[1] while no less than forty cushions were listed. These had coverings of velvet, gilt leather, sewed worsted, sewed silk and applied cloth of gold.

A hundred years later, wooden chairs with seats and backs up-holstered in Turkey work were to be found. Pieces survive in Holyroodhouse, and in the possession of the Merchant Company of Edinburgh. Turkey work is not strictly needlework. The pile is believed to have been knotted on to a base during weaving in the same way as in Oriental carpets.[2] There is no record of its being made commercially in Scotland as it was in England, where an undated petition, apparently presented during the reign of William and Mary, states that there were yearly made "and Vended in this Kingdom above five thousand dozen of SET WORK (commonly called Turkey Work Chairs, though made in England)".[3] It was not

67

a difficult technique to master, provided a small loom could be set up. Even a large piece of Turkey work could be made, such as the Mary Erskine table carpet, belonging to the Merchant Company of Edinburgh. This measures 246 cm. by 178 cm. (97 inches by 70 inches), and there seems no reason to doubt the traditional view that it was made by the first pupils of the Merchant Maiden Hospital, under supervision (Plate 39).

The irregularities in spelling and lettering make it unlikely that it was a professional piece. The table carpet bears the inscription: "To the Merchant Maiden Hospital. He that Giveth to the poor lendeth to the Lord that which He will pay him again. The Lord's our shepherd we will no wante, the feare of the Lord is the on thign. Founded by 50 Merchants and Mary Arskene, 1710." Mary Erskine, widow of John Hair, merchant and druggist, made a donation in 1694 of 10,000 merks (1 merk = 13s. 4d. Scots, = 4s. sterling) to found a school, the Merchant Maiden Hospital, now the Mary Erskine School. The Merchant Company and others added to this sum and the school was established until 1702 in the Great Lodgings of the Company's Hall in the Cowgate, Edinburgh. Mary Erskine died in 1707. In places where the dark brown wool of the carpet has rotted, owing to the dyestuff used, it has been repaired in a Gobelin stitch.

By 1710, table carpets might have been considered a little old-fashioned in England, but their use continued in the Low Countries, where the Edinburgh merchants still had close ties.

One other comparable carpet in Turkey work is known to have survived. It is dated 1746 and was made and signed by two English sisters, Ann Nevill and Parnel Nevill; each sister did one side, presumably sitting side by side at the loom. The line of demarcation wavers down the middle. It is 236 cm. by 208 cm. (93 inches by 82 inches), a little squarer than the Mary Erskine carpet, it is not clear if it was intended as a floor or a table carpet. It is now in the George Washington Museum, Mount Vernon.

Embroidered chair seats, like embroidered table carpets, were more within the scope of the domestic needlewoman than Turkey work, with its exacting counting out of each knot to build up the design, line by line, which resulted in stiffly geometrical flowers.

Tent or cross stitch on canvas could depict far more fluently the curves of leaves or drapery. Stuffed and upholstered chairs began to be popular at the beginning of the eighteenth century. The traditional velvet and leather were still used as coverings, to be succeeded as the century wore on by lighter, less durable materials, silks and printed chintz, and, for the wealthy, tapestry coverings imported mainly from France. Undeterred by changes in taste, the domestic needlewoman continued to make needlework covers for chairs and settees. Large sets were undertaken: unmounted ones still survive and reveal a startling intensity of colour. A set belonging to Lord Crawford which was brought to Balcarres from Haigh Hall, Lancashire, was made early in the eighteenth century. It has rural and classical figures in 34 medallions, and comprises covers for chair seats, a settee, and also what appear to be panels for a screen. It has been rolled up, unused, since the time it was finished, and the strong blues, yellows and reds dispel the widely held belief that the vegetable dyes used in the eighteenth century were gentle and subtle. A set of twelve chair seats at Gosford House, belonging to Lord Wemyss, has a flower design on a white background. They were used to cover ten chairs; but two covers (Plate 40) remain unused, and the edge shows that they were intended for chairs of a different shape from those on which they are now used. An unused incomplete set, also at Gosford, shows a bowl of flowers on a golden yellow ground worked in silk (Plate 41).

Today, an embroidered cover is made to refurbish an old chair. It is difficult for us to appreciate that in the eighteenth century the chairs were frequently made for the covers. A large set of covers took a considerable time to make, but it was not difficult to order a set of chairs from a cabinet maker. The very wealthy man of taste, could, when we were not at war with France, commission tapestry covers and then order chairs to be made for them. The sixth Earl of Coventry, of Croome Court, Worcestershire, went to France in 1763, at the end of the Seven Years War, and ordered a set of tapestry wall hangings from the Gobelins factory, together with a set of covers for six chairs and two settees, with a design of bouquets of flowers on a magnificent crimson ground. The order was completed in 1771, by which time Lord Coventry had secured

Robert Adam to design a room for the tapestries. The room with the tapestries and furniture is now in the Metropolitan Museum, New York.[4] "6 Large Antique Elbow Chairs with oval Backs carv'd with Double husks and ribbon knot on top, Gilt in the Best Burnish'd Gold, Stuffed with Best hair, in Linen—Backt with Fine Crimson Tammy—proper for covering with Tapestry in the Country" (Plate 42), cost £77 8s. 0d. The two settees cost £56 10s. 0d. They were made by Mayhew and Ince, London, and covered at Croome Court by three of their workmen, who also put up the wall tapestries.

For the more thrifty, or those with larger houses to furnish, a set of chair seats could be made at home by the wife and daughters, the governess (like May Menzies) and any female who could wield a needle. At Blair Castle, Perthshire, the second Duke of Atholl ordered a set of eight handsome mahogany chairs (Plate 43) with fish-scale carving on the legs, for which he supplied the seats and backs, embroidered with cornucopiae and flowers, apparently worked by his second wife, Jean Drummond, whom he had married in 1749. The bill for the chairs, made by William Gordon, London and dated June 17th, 1756, was for the sum of £31 8s. 0d. There was also a charge of £2 5s. 0d. "to making an addition to your Grace's needlework".[5] Anyone who has worked a chair seat will sympathize with the Duchess: too much background means that the upholsterer cuts the stitches when turning it in to cover the seat. Too little, as in this case, results in bare canvas showing unless someone fills in the ground.

The Duke of Atholl's daughter and heiress, Charlotte, married her cousin, John Murray of Strowan, the son of Lord John Murray who had lost his right of succession to the Dukedom for his part in the rising of 1745. Charlotte's husband, John Murray of Strowan, succeeded in place of his father and became 3rd Duke of Atholl. Charlotte, who may have helped her stepmother with the set of eight chairs, is believed to have worked the covers for another splendid set of twelve chairs and two settees with bolster cushions. Like the Croome Court set, each has a bouquet of flowers (in this case, moss roses and oak leaves) but is set against a white ground now mellowed to a silvery cream, and wreathed with a ribbon, worked in long and short stitch (Plate 44). The charge for the first chair was three guineas: added to this was an extra: ". . . white worsted and making out the ground of the needlework . . . 8s." The chair was japanned, but this was not apparently acceptable, and the set delivered in 1783 was gilded.[6]

Throughout the whole of the eighteenth century, France set the fashion in sets of tapestry chair covers, but the style was international, and all over Europe flowered chair seats were worked in wool and silk on canvas, usually in tent stitch with cross stitch at the edge to give extra wear. They still survive, from Spain to Scandinavia, from Dublin to Dresden. To label the design of an embroidered chair seat *Chippendale* or *Sheraton* because it happens to have been found on a chair by a particular cabinet maker, is misleading. The purchaser or his architect decided the design, not the cabinet maker. Apart from floral designs, many of them have medallions or panels showing mythological or rural scenes or figures in costume. The designs, as before, were taken from printed sources: book illustrations, costume prints, or occasionally ornamental engravings, intended for embroiderers and others. Martin Engelbrecht (1684–1756) in Augsburg published small designs expressly for embroiderers: the Four Continents, vases of flowers, birds and other scenes.

A set of chairs, with a settee, which were at Newhailes, Midlothian when Doctor Johnson visited there on his celebrated tour, and are still there, are said to have been worked by Lady Christian Hamilton, who married Sir James Dalrymple in 1725. One of the chairs shows a man with a tray and a girl in a high crowned hat on either side of an orange tree (Plate 45). The female figure is taken from a plate in a book of peasant costume published in Amsterdam in 1728: *Diverses Modes* illustrated by Bernard Picart, the plate shows a peasant girl from Brabant holding a stick of spitted larks or quails for sale (Plate 46). A Dutch version was published in which there was a male and female figure, it may be that the chair seat is derived directly from this.[7]

Engraved sources for other chair seats have been identified.[8] One of a pair of carved mahogany chairs in the Victoria and Albert Museum shows *Le Soir* from *Pastorale no. 12* after Jacques Stella, engraved by his niece Claudine (Bouzonnet) and published in Paris in 1667. Another chair (Victoria and Albert Museum W.25–1922) has scenes taken from Ogilby's Virgil illustrated by Cleyn, published in London in 1654. Scenes from this book also furnished the designs on the screen panels worked by Lady Juiia Calverley at Wallington, Northumberland in 1727.[9] A wing chair, in the Untermyer collection, New York, shows the figure of Harlequin taken from an engraving published by Nicholas Bonnart (1636–1718). A chair in the Lady Lever Art Gallery, Port Sunlight, shows the *Judgement of Solomon* from an engraving by B. A. Bolswert (1580–1633) after Rubens. As in the case of the Mellerstain panel, most of the engravings had been published upwards of fifty years or more before they were chosen as embroidery designs.

These pictorial chairs, and indeed most of the floral designs, are very competently drawn out on the canvas which indicates that they were executed by a trained draughtsman, who had an engraving before him to copy. So far as is known, no evidence has yet emerged to show that these chair covers could be bought ready traced. But it is significant that in 1738, in Massachusetts, an advertisement inserted by a Mrs. Condy advised readers that they could obtain from her "all sorts of beautiful figures on canvas, for Tent Stick; the Patterns from London, but drawn by her much cheaper than English drawing; all sorts of canvas, without drawing; also . . . Cruells of all sorts, the best White Chapple Needles, and everything for all Sorts of Work".[10] Perhaps in country districts in Britain a visiting artist or draughtsman drew out the designs on to the canvas. Lady Grisell Baillie employed the Edinburgh artist, John Scougal (*c*. 1645–1730) and paid him £6 4*s*. 0*d*. for two pictures and frames, and another £4 for other pictures.[11] She added to her accounts . . . "For drawing Grisie's peticoat by Scougald . . . 5/- stg." This was in 1706, the year the panel was completed by her two daughters, and the year that the "satin pece" was begun. The motifs on the Mellerstain panel were traced directly from May Menzies's book which no doubt also provided the designs on the "satin pece". A larger, more flowing design may have been required for the petticoat, but it is idle to surmise the type of embroidery chosen. However, the technique and the shading of the

Mellerstain panel show that pictorial subjects were well within the competence even of young girls, working under their governess. More experienced needlewomen would have no difficulty in working the figures with their drapery, once they were drawn out on canvas.

From the middle of the eighteenth century, pleasing and durable covers were made in cross stitch in geometrical or scale patterns, simply counted out on the canvas like knitting patterns. Two are at Newhailes; an armchair at Mellerstain which still survives in good condition was included in a portrait of 1828, and a rather worn example of this type of needlework can be seen at Wordsworth's Cottage, Grasmere, associated with Dorothy. Florentine stitch in graduated shades was also used and may have been more common than we now imagine, as it is less durable than cross stitch. An interesting pair of square samplers for chair seats (Plate 47), now mounted in a two-leaved fire screen are to be found at Lauriston Castle, Edinburgh. They are undated, but show a central flower-piece within a border of counted patterns, one cross stitch, one Florentine on each sampler. They are true samplers, that is, a pattern record, not a trial of technique.

REFERENCES

1. THOMSON, T. [ed.], *Collection of inventories of the Royal Wardrobe and Jewelhouse*, Edinburgh, 1815, pp. 212–14.

2. TATTERSALL, C. E. C., *A History of British Carpets*, F. Lewis, Benfleet 1934, p. 58.

3. Quoted by G. TOWNSEND, *Needle and Bobbin Club Bulletin*, 1944, Vol. 28, no. 102, p. 4.

4. See PARKER, J., and STANDEN, E., *Metropolitan Museum of Art Bulletin*, New York, Nov. 1959.

5. COLERIDGE, A., "Chippendale, the Director and some Cabinet Makers at Blair Castle," *Connoisseur*, Vol. CXLVI, Dec. 1960, p. 252.

6. COLERIDGE, A., "The 3rd and 4th Dukes of Atholl and the Firm of Chipchase Cabinet Makers," *Connoisseur*, Vol. CLXI, Feb. 1966, p. 97.

7. I am indebted to Dr. M. A. H. Crol, Atlas van Stolk Foundation, Rotterdam, for identifying this figure.

8. Identified by Mrs. Nancy Groves Cabot, who has kindly allowed me to use this information.

9. WINGFIELD DIGBY, G., *Connoisseur*, Vol. CXLV, 1960. p.169

10. Quoted by G. TOWNSEND, *Bulletin of the Museum of Fine Arts, Boston*, Dec. 1942, pp. 111–15.

11. *The Household Book of Lady Grisell Baillie 1672–1733*, Scottish History Society, 1911, p. xxvi.

Samplers

Needlework samplers, especially of cross-stitch designs, still survive in large numbers, kept no doubt for sentimental reasons, they have survived because most of them were glazed and framed. The fashion for collecting them began apparently around the turn of this century.[1] They are quaint and decorative and are probably the most easily displayed pieces of historical domestic needlework. The verses, often from the hymns of Charles Wesley, and the fact that they are usually signed and often dated, with the tender age of the worker added, increase their human interest.

Samplers have been dealt with exhaustively by so many other writers,[2] that it might seem superfluous to try to add anything to what has already been written, but in a book that stresses the printed sources of design, some discussion of samplers and their uses is indispensable.

It is always assumed that originally a needlework sampler (*exemplar*) was a record of patterns as well as stitches, and because of this it was treasured and bequeathed by will.[3] This assumption has yet to be proved, since no sampler worked before the first publication of printed pattern books in the sixteenth century has so far been found. Samplers as we know them appear to be more a record of technique than a dictionary of design. Very few of the single motifs, or the strips of geometrical stylized flowers seen on early samplers, can be found on any other completed embroidery that has survived. In the Carew-Pole collection, a sampler shows a linked hexagon diaper design, which can be seen on two completed cushion covers in the same house. These cushion covers were considered by A. J. B. Wace to be sixteenth-century work.[4] The sampler design is incomplete, enclosing a different flower from that found on the cushion covers. It may be that this piece of linen, on which there are other incomplete designs, is a true sampler: that is, a record of designs gathered by the worker for her future use, like a recipe book in cookery. On the other hand, it looks remarkably like the kind of trial piece that many needlewomen even today keep in their workboxes, to try out the best way of working a stitch or design before embarking on the actual work. A man's cap at Drummond Castle, Perthshire, has been preserved with the legal and Thistle robes worn by James, 4th Earl of Perth, Lord Chancellor of Scotland in 1684. The cap, worked with silk and silver thread on linen, is covered with 'S' devices of a type often found on seventeenth-century samplers. It may be that these sampler patterns were used more than we are now apt to think, on household linen or clothing that has long since disintegrated.

Where embroidery or lace was worked to order, however, it was necessary to have completed specimens of selected designs to show to customers. These trade samplers, with motifs which are often numbered and could be ordered, or used as the basis of a special design to order, are not easy to find. They were rarely preserved after their original use was ended, as unlike children's samplers they seldom made satisfactory wall decorations, and lacked sentimental appeal. Professional embroiderers must always have used these worked examples, as well as sketches, to show to customers and for the reference of workers. One of these samplers, a width of white muslin, 72·8 cm. wide by 208·5 cm. long (28½ inches by 82 inches), with about thirty numbered designs, worked mostly in chain stitch with a tambour hook, came from Old Cumnock, Ayrshire, in the first decade of the nineteenth century. On it are worked handkerchief corners, skirt flounces, borders and all-over trellis and sprig designs.[5] These designs, they are literally embroidered samples, were worked on a loom width of muslin stretched on a large frame with heavy rollers to hold it taut, at which two girls could sit, one on either side. The muslin was made in Scotland, in imitation of Indian muslin, and the tambour embroidery which was undertaken by young girls, became immensely popular and fashionable at the end of the eighteenth and the first two decades of the nineteenth centuries.

Another trade sampler came also from Ayrshire, but is slightly later in date.[6] It consists of eighty needlepoint fillings, worked in differently shaped spaces, in lines of eight, each numbered in ink. This was a worker's sampler of about 1830–1850, of the type of embroidery now called *Ayrshire needlework*, a later development of the tamboured muslin of the previous sampler. This embroidery, unlike tamboured muslin, was not worked on a frame in a workroom, but given out, mostly to country women who worked it in their own homes. It was collected and paid for by agents, working for manufacturers in Glasgow and Paisley, who made up, and marketed the baby robes, caps, women's dresses, collars and cuffs ornamented with this delicate white embroidery.

Irish linen manufacturers also used these trade samplers. A book of over a hundred handkerchief initials enclosed in different designs survives from a Belfast firm of the nineteenth century. The handkerchiefs were given out, like Ayrshire embroidery, to workers in their own homes.

Until recently, worked designs for bed and table linen could be seen in Belfast and London shops, with a designer on hand to sketch out variations. French and other continental linen shops also had selections from which customers could choose designs to be worked in the linen or silk of their choice. Regimental and ecclesiastical embroiderers still use these trade samplers. They must, of course, have been used in needlework workrooms of the eighteenth century and earlier, but were not deemed worthy of preservation.

Schoolchildren's samplers, on the other hand, abound in Britain, boys' as well as girls', especially of the eighteenth and nineteenth centuries. As might be expected in these, which are small practice-pieces in a chosen technique, old-fashioned motifs, like nursery rhymes learnt by the teacher in her youth, tended to linger on longer than other forms of embroidery. It may be remembered, however, that except in dress, up-to-date designs were not greatly valued. Engravings were often utilized for a chair seat or hanging fifty or a hundred years after they were first published.

It is not surprising that so many samplers should have survived, for they played an indispensable part in a little girl's education, and could be used to teach sewing and the alphabet in one exercise. Lady Nithsdale, who rescued her husband from the Tower of London on the eve of his execution for his part in the Jacobite rising of 1715, by dressing him in women's clothes and passing him off as her attendant, spent the rest of her life in penurious exile in Paris and Rome. Three years after her husband's escape, she wrote to her sister-in-law, the Countess of Traquair, from Paris, about the education of her little daughter, Lady Anne Maxwell: ". . . especially having the child to provide for in daily necessarys; and masters, of whom she has 4, a dancing master, a singing master, a harpsicall master, and French master, for since perhaps she may never have wherwithall to portion her, she stands more in need of good qualitys, so that I am willing to squeese it out, even out of necessarys to myselfe, thinking her education preferable to my wants, except what is unavoidable to keep life and soul together. She learns to write, but [for] that I content myself with Evansis (Lady Nithsdale's maid) hand. But between all these her day is pretty well employd; for she has her English reading, and her sampler, and has done already the 24 letters twice over, both sides alike, and all her masters are satisfy'd with her."[7] At this time Lady Anne was not quite five years old.

Some typical samplers show how conservative was the choice of motif, and how comprehensive was the training in various types of needlework. The sampler of Betty Plenderleath (worked under the direction of Mrs. Seton who kept a school in Edinburgh), which is dated 1745 is in the Royal Scottish Museum (Plate 48). It shows many motifs from previous centuries, Adam and Eve with the serpent under a stiffer tree than that of the Campbell of Glenorchy valance (see Plate 10) still occupies the central space; the caterpillar might have come from Thomas Johnson's book of 1630. The formal trees, hares and baskets of flowers are international, and can be found on German and Dutch samplers. The border of bold flowers at the top with twisted stem and fern-like leaf must have been extremely popular. It can be found on many samplers: there is one in the Fitzwilliam Museum, Cambridge, dated 1629, another in the Victoria and Albert Musuem of 1633 (T.194–1927), others in the same museum ((443–1884) of 1696), ((1017–1905) of 1651), ((804–1877) of 1656), as well as several undated examples. It can be recognized in samplers in many private collections, and persisted till the middle of the nineteenth century, when it can have had no use save as a technical exercise in the counting out of a cross-stich pattern. The peacock on Betty Plenderleath's sampler, with its six (in other cases there are sometimes seven) circular tail feathers, has been regarded as a peculiarly Scottish motif.[8] Although it can rarely be found on English samplers, it is common on Scandinavian samplers of the period, particularly Danish. It also appears on a much earlier piece: a Burse in the Victoria and Albert Museum, of about 1290–1340 (1416–1874). In the two lower corners of Betty Plenderleath's sampler can be seen geometrical cross-stitch designs, suitable for chair seats when worked in wool on a coarser canvas, with a Florentine pattern between the two lions.

Perhaps the best way to illustrate how samplers were used to develop technique is shown in the four worked by Elizabeth Gardner, of Glasgow, between 1818 and 1822. It will be remembered that Martha Edlin, born in 1660, completed four pieces of needlework between 1668 and 1673. She completed a sampler with alphabets at the age of eight and the following year made a white cutwork sampler. She then made a white satin raised work casket dated 1671 and in 1673 made a jewel case with beadwork, rococo and tent stitches.[9] All of them might be regarded as essays in different needlework techniques.

Elizabeth Gardner, daughter of Andrew Gardner, a mathematical optician of Candleriggs, Glasgow, was born in 1806, and completed her first sampler at the age of twelve (Plate 49). Like Martha Edlin's, it is a businesslike affair with alphabets, but worked in red and green worsted on open linen. It was a common enough sampler in Scotland, and if her others had not survived, it would not have merited a second glance. The red and green colouring, and the row of coronets crowning her parents' initials would have suggested a Scottish origin, even if she had not proudly embroidered GLASGOW 1818 below her name. The second alphabet in eyelet holes looks back to the day when laces, threaded through eyelet holes were more usual on undergarments than buttons. The heart in the curiously old-fashioned rococo stitch can be found on earlier samplers.

Elizabeth's second sampler, of 1820 (Plate 50) was worked in silk, not worsted, now faded to fawn and blue, though it may originally, like the first, have been red and green. It is a much more assured piece, but it is surprising to find double-running (Holbein) stitch patterns still being worked as late as 1820. The highly decorative alphabet is of the type that led Marcus Huish to ascribe a Scottish origin to an eighteenth-century sampler on account of "the bright colouring, coarsish canvas and ornate lettering".[10] The familiar peacocks regard each other beneath strawberries (or flowers) of rococo stitch on either side of a tree, with the initials of Elizabeth's parents beneath.

Her third sampler (Plate 51) was completed the following year, and as yet no parallel to it can be found among English samplers. It shows, worked loosely in red and green silk for clarity, some of the stitches and fillings used in so-called *Dresden work* or drawn muslin. This type of fine white embroidery, worked on a loosely woven muslin, was a type often taught in young ladies' schools of the period, and was used as a cheap but rather laborious imitation of pillow or needlepoint lace, and could be used on aprons, shirt frills and caps. Many white samplers of Dresden work fillings are to be found in Scandinavia, especially in Copenhagen and Stockholm. Most of them are early nineteenth century, but the earliest is dated 1678 in the Nordiska Museet, Stockholm (127–541). This shows a similar basket filling to that on Elizabeth Gardner's sampler (Plate 52). Oddly, no white samplers of Dresden work have so far been found in Britain, although advertisements for girls' schools in the late eighteenth century, particularly in Scotland, show that this type of embroidery was taught to young ladies. This red and green sampler demonstrates that the stitches were learnt, and could be taught, using a coarser canvas and coloured thread. The Royal Scottish Museum has an undated example of the same type as Elizabeth Gardner's, also in red and green (1956–1195), and the Ulster Museum, Belfast, has one dated

Plate 35. Casket by Hannah Smith 1654–1656. She wrote a note, enclosed in the casket to remind herself of when it was made: 'I went to Oxford in the year 1654 . . . . . and I came away in 1656, and I was almost 12 years of age, when I made an end of my cabbinet . . .' The front door panel shows Deborah and Barak, and (right) Jael and Sisera. On the sides are Autumn (Ceres) and Winter, a man warming himself at a fire.

Coloured silks, gilt and silver thread on white satin. The lion and leopard are in raised work.

Fine tent and rococo stitch with seed pearls and laid stitch.

The Whitworth Art Gallery, University of Manchester

Plate 36. Lid of casket by Hannah Smith. Joseph being raised from the pit and sold to the Midianite merchants, (Genesis XXXVII 28). The figures of Joseph and the two men raising him, together with the bundle and staff, are taken, in mirror image, from an engraving by Gerard de Jode.
Laid stitches in silk with metal thread. The figure on the right has a coat worked in detached lace stitches. 17·7 × 25·4 cm.
The Whitworth Art Gallery, University of Manchester

Infidijs circumuentum, putroque profundo Extractum vendunt, idque petente Ruben. Gene. 37.

Plate 37. Engraving by Gerard de Jode. Joseph being raised from the pit. *From Thesaurus Sacrarum Historiaru Veteris Testamenti.* Antwerp 1585. 19 × 28 cm.
National Library of Scotland

Plate 38. Lower half of sampler signed and dated Mary Lawley 1667. Floral patterns in rows, with the padded figure of a woman, wearing gown and blue stole of detached lace stitches.

Silk and metal threads on linen.

Cross, satin, chain, double-running and lace stitches.

Mr. Gervase Riddell-Carre

Plate 39. The Mary Erskine table carpet. Turkey work, extensively repaired with Gobelin stitch. Panel of red flowers in groups of four, surrounded by inscription: HE THAT GIVETH TO THE POOR LENDETH TO THE LORD THAT WHICH HE WILL PAY HIM AGAIN. THE LORD'S OUR SHEPHERD WE WILL NOT WANTE, THE FEARE OF THE LORD IS THE ON THIGN. FOUNDED BY 50 MERCHANTS AND MARY ARSKINE. 1710. M.A.   About 228 × 177 cm.

The Master's Court of the Company of Merchants of the City of Edinburgh

1793, which is, presumably, Irish. Another exists in a private collection.

Elizabeth's fourth and last sampler, dated 1822, when she was sixteen, is a small white one, 12·7 cm. (5 inches) square, outlined with dark blue satin ribbon (Plate 53). It is of a type fairly common in Scotland, and the ribbon frame, with bows at the corners, is found on many Scandinavian samplers of the period. It has four squares of darning patterns, imitations of common weaves of linen damask, useful in repairing table linen. "Suites of linen" – table-cloths and napkins, are listed in eighteenth-century Scottish inventories in a variety of weaves: *rose knot, lavender knot*, the *Walls of Troy* and *burdseye*.[11] Five other small squares on the sampler show needlepoint lace fillings, of the same type as those on the Ayrshire needlework trade sampler already mentioned. The circular Hollie point medallion, with initials and date contrived by leaving spaces in the tightly knotted rows, was still being used for the crowns of babies' caps, but would shortly be replaced by the more varied needlepoint crowns of Ayrshire needlework. Having completed her four samplers, Elizabeth Gardner had learnt a useful variety of needlework and lace stitches.

REFERENCES

1. HUISH, M., *Samplers and Tapestry Embroideries*, Longmans Green, London, 1900.

2. For example:
   ASHTON, LEIGH, *Samplers*, Medici Society, London, 1926.
   COLBY, A., *Samplers*, Batsford, London, 1964.
   HUISH, M., *Samplers and Tapestry Embroideries*, Longmans Green, London, 1900.
   JONES, M. E., *British Samplers*, Pen in Hand, Oxford, 1948.
   KING, D., *Samplers*, Victoria and Albert Museum, 1960.
   ODDY, R., *Samplers in Guildford Museum*, Guildford, 1951.

3. *Essex Review*, XVII, 1908, p. 147.

4. WACE, A. J. B., *English embroideries belonging to Sir John Carew-Pole, Bart.*, Walpole Society, Vol. XXI, 1933, p. 43.

5. Now belonging to James Finlay and Co. Ltd., Glasgow.

6. In the collection of Miss S. Morris, Ayr. Illustrated in SWAIN, M. H., "Two Rare Scottish Samplers", *Embroidery*, Spring 1960, Vol. XI, no. 1.

7. *The Book of Caerlavrock* privately printed Edinburgh, 1875. Letter 239, Nov. 14th, 1717, p. 165.

8. FOTHERGILL, G. A., "Notes on Scottish Samplers", *Proc. of the Soc. of Antiquaries of Scotland*, Vol. XLIII, March 8th, 1908.

9. Victoria and Albert, no. T41 – 1954, (Jewel case). The other articles are on loan to the museum.

10. HUISH, M., op. cit., pl. XVIII.

11. DUNBAR, E. D., *Social life in former days chiefly in the Province of Moray*, Edmondston & Douglas, Edinburgh, 1865, p. 205.

Embroidered Lace

The lace stitches seen on Scottish samplers lasting until well into the nineteenth century are no accident. They reflect the constant effort of the native needlewoman to provide fine lace, which would otherwise have had to be imported. The merchants who traded with the Low Countries may well have smuggled in a great deal of undeclared lace for their wives and daughters; curiously, the Calvinist church does not seem to have frowned on white lace, and only lack of money and a native lace industry prevented the wives of Scottish burghers from following the fashion of their Calvinist sisters in Holland, who are portrayed in rich crisply starched white lace.

Efforts to establish a lace industry in Scotland were never very successful because the fine linen thread required had always to be imported. A strenuous attempt was made during the eighteenth century to subsidize and encourage a native linen industry. Superior flax seed was imported from Riga, and premiums paid to growers. Spinning schools were established, and, while a useful amount of sewing thread was produced, nothing could compare with the fine thread spun in France and the Low Countries for continental lace makers. At least three attempts were made to establish Scottish pillow lace, all of them from philanthropic motives. The Duchess of Hamilton, the beautiful Anne Gunnings, started a lace school at Hamilton in 1725 for twelve poor girls aged seven who were kept till they were fourteen, but the lace produced was coarse and unremarkable. Similarly, in 1815 a gold medal was presented by the Board of Trustees for Agriculture and Manufactures to Lady Ramsay of Balmain for founding a Lace School at Montrose, but nothing more is heard of it.[1] Around 1850, the Rev. William Webster, rector of the Episcopal church of New Pitsligo, Aberdeenshire, started a local industry in a parish which had few natural resources, and lace, similar in pattern to that made in the east midlands of England, is still made there by a few enthusiastic amateurs.

In all these schools, pillow or bobbin lace was taught; this requires, not only expertise, but equipment, bobbins and pillows, fine even thread, and a designer to supply the pricked designs. Left to themselves, the workers would happily go on reproducing the old designs, but in transferring a worn-out pricking to a new piece of parchment, some of the detail was apt to get lost, and the design degenerated and became blurred. The best of the continental lace schools avoided this by employing professional designers, and it was the design, as well as the superlative fineness of continental lace, that made those who could afford it, in Scotland as well as the rest of Britain, continue to pay for imported lace, with or without the customs dues that resulted in the Porteus riots of 1736.

The careful Lady Grisell Baillie did not stint money on lace for her daughter Grisell's trousseau when she married Alexander Murray in August 1710:

	Sterling		
	£	s	d
For a head sute fine laces to Grisie, £10. 9. 9. ruffles £5. 8.	15	17	9
For lace to shift tuckers and egins etc.	15	6	0
For Grisie's best night cloathes and ruffles	3	12	0
For a headsute of narrow lace to Grisie and ruffles	4	10	6
For lace for tuckers and egin	2	10	0
For fine muslin for Grisie's apron and heads etc.	1	14	0
For ruffles to Rachy's fine head	2	11	0[2]

Grisell had no children: her husband had a violent temper and in 1714 they were separated by decree. Her sister Rachel married in 1717 Lord Binning, eldest son of the Earl of Haddington and for the arrival of her first grandchild in 1718, Lady Grisell indulged in an orgy of spending:

EMBROIDERED LACE

	Sterling		
	£	s	d
August 16th 1718 My Rachy's childs clothes			
To Mrs. Lindsay in full	1	0	0
For scouring gowns		12	0
For mending lace 5s, a book 1s		6	0
For child bed linen and everything she wanted	74	4	3
Nov. 19 For egine Mrs. Tempest	1	4	0
For ½ piece jueling for child's day vests		16	0
For cleaning a gown py'd Whitsun		4	0
For quilting a gown	1	10	0
For 2 baskets		6	0
For little wastcoats 3s		3	0
For 4 p. little threed Mittons		2	6
For Mrs. Child's account coats and frocks	4	11	6
For holland from Lind	4	19	0
For 6 sute little linens besides the egines	4	15	0
For Mrs. Perks for egins for 3 suts	5	15	9
For a Bed table and chair from Moor	1	10	0
For more eggins	1	10	0
For 4¼ yd. Podisoy for a cloak	2	13	0
For scarlet sesnet at 3.6	1	0	0
For making the clock the lace my own		4	0
For more eggine		11	6

Some of the edging bought so prodigally by Lady Grisell may have been silk fringes, but the six suits of small linen, for instance, and the four pairs of baby mittens, many of which survive, were undoubtedly trimmed with white lace.

Britain was not alone in imposing import dues on lace, or when necessary banning its import altogether. In 1714 the two eldest daughters of the 4th Earl of Traquair were sent, at the ages of eighteen and seventeen, to a Paris convent to complete their education. They received visits from their Jacobite and Catholic relatives and friends, and wrote to their mother in Scotland: ". . . There is nothing wee have more need of than a tolerable head (of lace) to goe out with, for wee have but each of one, and we want another to chinge with it."[3] And later, "If your Ladyship thinks fitt to send the lace for our head clothes, 'em that brings it must take care to hid it, for it is a thing that is forbidden here. . . . We will not get a tolerable lace here under 20 livers an ell." (About thirty shillings a yard.)[4]

It is not surprising, therefore, that many women should attempt to make their own lace with a needle and thread. Bobbin lace required skill and implements, but true needlepoint required only the mastering of different looped stitches, so arranged that the holes between the loops form different patterns, to make the filling or *réseau*. A fine thread was also required, and this had to be imported, but a small amount would make a considerable length of edging for a collar or infant's shirt. In 1622 the family of Lord William Howard, of Naworth Castle, Northumberland, sent to London for "sisters threed" (*filum sororum* : a lace thread made in convents of Flanders and Italy), and again in 1630 paid 12 pence for "one ounce of Nunn's threed", though a considerable amount of *bone lace* (bobbin lace) was bought as well.[5]

The earliest type of needle-made lace, *cutwork*, was made from cut or fringed linen, the threads of which formed the foundation on which the designs were worked in darning or looped stitches. The winding sheet of St. Cuthbert, when his body was disinterred on August 29th, 1104, had a decorated border which sounds remarkably like cutwork judging from the minute description given by Reginald of Durham :

> This sheet had fringes of linen thread on either side, for the sheet was without doubt made of linen. Moreover . . . there was a border at the edge, worked by the skilful art of the same weaver. And on this material a very fine embroidery stands out a little from the strands of the thread, which is found to contain the shapes of birds and beasts. Always, however, between two pairs of birds or beasts there appears a woven figure like a tree in full leaf, which divides and separates their shapes on either side, and so by disjoining them makes them distinct. The shapely figure of the tree also, thus portrayed, is seen to spread out its leaves, tiny as they may be, on both sides. And immediately

86

beneath them in similar fashion embroidered forms of animals.
. . . This cloth was removed from the sacred body at the time of
its translation, and was long preserved intact in the church as a
covering for the gifts of relics which are daily exhibited to the
faithful.[6]

Later, laid linen threads attached to parchment acted as a foundation for the needlework fillings, instead of cut or fringed linen.
The earliest printed pattern books, published in Germany and Italy
in the sixteenth century, contained designs, not for coloured surface
embroidery, but for lace patterns for cutwork of this type, and also
for darned net, called *filet* or *lacis*. The knotted net, which served
as a foundation for lacis, was made in the same way as fishermen's
nets, and then stretched on a square metal frame to make each
mesh square. The resulting spaces were darned or left blank to
form intricate designs. Lacis was a type of lace known to Mary
Queen of Scots. The Italian, Vinciolo, had dedicated his book of
printed designs to her mother-in-law, Catherine de Medici, in 1587.
At her own request, Mary was supplied with netting needles and
gauges for making knotted netting when in captivity on the island
of Lochleven (see Chapter 3). In 1578, among the items listed in
Edinburgh Castle, were eight small pieces of knotted netting, but
made in silk, not as was more usual, in linen, with "a design begun
to sew on & not perfite". But apart from the Queen of Scots, with
her French–Italian education, Lacis does not appear to have been so
popular in Britain as cutwork on linen. White samplers of the
seventeenth century in Britain show elaborate patterns of cutwork,
many of them deriving from the German and Italian printed
pattern books. The samplers show a high degree of workmanship,
and are often combined with geometrical satin stitch counted by
the thread and worked in white linen thread on linen.

Another early form of needlework lace is *hollie* (perhaps Holy)
point, a circle of which contains the initials and date on Elizabeth
Gardner's fourth sampler of 1822 (see Plate 53). The holes, which
have given to it its name, left in the tightly knotted rows, form
letters, flowers or figures. Hollie point is said to date from Tudor
times in Britain, but few references to it have been found. Among

the clothing left behind in Edinburgh by Mary Queen of Scots, and listed in 1578, was "ane collar of hollie crisp (crisp was a gauze-like material) with incarnat silk and silver".[7]

An unfinished sampler, mounted on vellum, consisting of sixty-eight worked squares of a surprising variety of needlepoint fillings, belonging to Dr. Douglas Goodhart, has an oblong panel of hollie point inscribed MARY QUELCH 1609 (Plate 54). This appears to be not only the earliest white sampler to have survived, but the earliest dated example of hollie point. The Campbell inventory of 1640 lists ". . . Holland scheittis 2 pair quhairof 1 pair schewit with hollie work".[8] The Fitzwilliam Museum, Cambridge, has two samplers showing hollie point, one dated 1679, another 1711. The sampler of Jenny Grant (Plate 55) dated 1724 and 1725 shows several patterns in this stitch, combined with well-executed square designs like seventeenth-century cutwork, as well as circles filled with the needlepoint *wheels* so beloved in nineteenth-century white-work. Her sampler is worked with great precision. The arrangement, and even the fillings, have been found on several samplers dated within the succeeding ten years. They are so close in design that they would seem to stem from a common source.

Some of the detached coloured lace found on raised work figures also looks remarkably like hollie point (see Chapter 8). If these caskets and panels are to be regarded generally as schoolgirls' pieces, the detached garments, and the toys and flowers often found inside, may be samples of different lace fillings, executed in coloured silk for variety and interest, instead of white thread. Certainly white hollie point remained a favourite trimming for infant clothes and caps until the first quarter of the nineteenth century. Lady Grisell Baillie's edgings on the six little suits of linen for Rachel's baby were probably in this stitch. It is often found on the shirts and caps of an infant's layette, and dated examples can be found till the 1820's.

Lace made with fine thread and a needle was extremely slow and tedious to make, and for this reason the pieces of hollie point that remain are seldom very large or long. A more rapid and practical way of decorating caps and aprons in the home was by means of Dresden work, or as it was called in France, *point de Saxe*, or *point*

Plate 40. Unused chair seat, from a set of twelve, of which ten have been used to cover chairs of two differing styles. Silk and wool on linen canvas. Tent stitch and cross stitch. Late 18th. or early 19th. century.

The Earl of Wemyss and March

Plate 41. Unused chair back, now a cushion cover, from a set comprising nine backs and two seats. Each design worked in different colours on gold silk background.

Coloured silks on linen canvas.

Tent and cross stitch. Early 18th. century.   60·9 × 45·7 cm.

The Earl of Wemyss and March

Plate 42. Gilt chair, made by Mayhew and Ince for the Tapestry Room at Croome Court for the sixth Earl of Coventry. Covers of Gobelins tapestry, with crimson ground. c. 1769. Chair completed 1771.

The Metropolitan Museum of Art, New York

Plate 43. Mahogany chair with fish scale carving, made by William Gordon for the second Duke of Atholl. Covers by Jean Drummond, the Duke's second wife. One of a set of eight.
Silk and wool on canvas. Fine tent stitch. 1756.
The Duke of Atholl

Plate 44. Gilt chair, made by Chipchase and Lambert for the third Duke of Atholl. Covers by his wife, Charlotte. From a set of twelve chairs and two settees with bolster cushions.
Silk and wool on canvas. Cross stitch and long and short stitch. 1783.

Plate 45. Chair from a set of ten with settee. Associated with Lady Christian Hamilton, who married Sir James Dalrymple in 1725. Wool on canvas.
Tent stitch. Mid 18th. century. Design taken from 'Paysanne de Brabant' by Picart.

Sir Mark Dalrymple, Bt.

Plate 46. 'Paysanne de Brabant', an engraving from *'Diverses Modes dessinees d'apres Nature'* by Bernard Picart, published Amsterdam 1728.

Atlas van Stolk Foundation, Rotterdam

Plate 47.
Cross and Floren-
tine stitches. Un-
dated. Probably mid
18th century.
*From a fire screen at
Louriston Castle,
Edinburgh*

Plate 48. Sampler signed
and dated Betty Plenderleath
1745 at Mrs. Setons. Mrs.
Eupham Seton was a schoolmistress in Edinburgh till
1752. The border of large
flowers at the top can be
seen on many samplers,
from 1629 till the middle of
the 19th century. The two
lower corners show geo-
metrical designs suitable for
chair seats (compare with
Plate 47).
Coloured silks on linen.
Cross, satin, Florentine,
double-running, rococo
stitches and eyelet holes.
32 × 22·5 cm. no.1939. 122.
Royal Scottish Museum

Plate 49. Sampler signed and dated Elizabeth Gardner, Glasgow 1818. Alphabets in red and green with family initials, coronets and digits.
Coloured silks on linen.
Cross stitch, eyelet holes and rococo stitch.
40·6 × 27·9 cm.
The Misses Muirhead

Plate 50. Sampler signed and dated Elizabeth Gardner 1820 Glasgow together with her parents' initials. Alphabets and digits with two rows of double-running (Holbein stitch) designs.
Coloured silks, perhaps red and green but now faded to blue and fawn, on linen.
Cross stitch, eyelet holes, rococo and double-running stitches.
24·1 × 15·3 cm.
The Misses Muirhead

Plate 51. Sampler signed and dated Elizabeth Gardner, Glasgow, 1821. Drawn fabric ('pulled') stitch fillings, suitable for Dresden work.
Red and green silks on linen.
Cross stitch, square stitch, and a variety of drawn fabric stitches. Compare the 'basket filling' with that on the Swedish sampler, Plate 52. 22·5 × 15·2 cm.
The Misses Muirhead

Plate 52. Sampler signed and dated C M S 1678. Drawn fabric ('pulled') stitch fillings, suitable for Dresden work (see Chapter 11). Swedish.
Fine white linen thread on fine muslin.
Geometrical satin stitch, coral, double back stitch ('shadow work') and a variety of drawn fabric stitches. Compare the 'basket filling' to the right of '78' with that in left lower corner of Elizabeth Gardner's 1821 sampler, Plate 51. 27·5 × 29 cm. no. 127.541.
Nordiska Museet, Stockholm

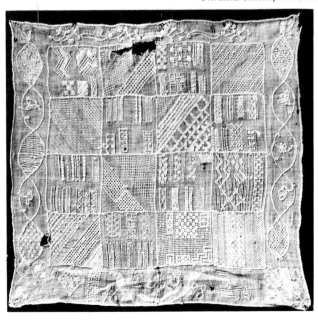

de Dinant. A woven ground of sheer, loosely woven cambric, or better still, Indian muslin, was used. This was tacked on to vellum on which a rococo lace design was drawn. The threads of the muslin were pulled together by fine stitches of varying patterns, to form the fillings.[9] Elizabeth Gardner's third sampler of 1821 shows these fillings as does the Swedish sampler of 1678 (see Plates 51 and 52). Dresden work is often erroneously labelled *Tônder Lace* in British museums. Tônder lace is, however, a pillow lace made in Denmark.

It is not known where Dresden work originated. The name suggests a Saxon origin, and certainly the technique, worked by counting threads on an evenly woven white ground, has certain similarities to the geometrical fillings of *Opus Teutonicum* worked on linen. Diderot, in his encyclopaedia of 1751, suggests it took the name of the country whose lace it imitated. By the time he compiled his encyclopaedia it was being made all over Europe, in Scandinavia as the sampler of 1678 (see Plate 52) shows, in Germany, France, the Low Countries, Britain, and even in New England. In Scotland a shirt ruffle exists, which is said to have been worn by Prince Charles Edward Stuart in 1745 (Plate 56). In 1758 the Burgh Council of Aberdeen appointed Miss Betsy Forbes, a schoolmistress of the city, being satisfied "as to her strict morality, Dresden work, and catgut lace making".[10] In New England, Rachel Leonard, of Norton, Massachusetts, worked a triangular kerchief for herself in this technique and fortunately for posterity finished it by including her initials and the date 1752[11] (Plate 57). She was then twenty-five years old, which we know because she had also worked a coat of arms which is still in existence, with her name and age: RACHEL LEONARD aged 13 1740.

It is clear that Dresden work was a thoroughly international fashion, and although the ruffles and aprons could be worked at home by the diligent needlewoman, a great deal was made for sale, especially on the continent of Europe. Travellers report buying "ruffles at Spaw", and Lady Mary Coke sent muslin to Hanover to be worked. The standard of the pieces that survive varies understandably from the crudely amateur to the elegantly professional. It was sufficiently prized, in some cases, to be remounted, when frequent laundering had worn away the plain muslin. An

89

advertisement on December 18th, 1772 in the *York Chronicle and Weekly Advertiser* told readers that, "Mrs. Richardson (Colliergate, York) . . . grafts old Dresden on new muslin so as not to be perceived where done . . ."

Few needlewomen followed Rachel Leonard's admirable example, and only a few dated pieces of Dresden work survive. These include an apron inscribed MARY TYRELL IN THE 14th YEAR OF HER AGE 1717 (Victoria and Albert Museum, 1564–1904), a panel with a vase of flowers inscribed M. BRADBURY 1733 (Victoria and Albert Museum, Lewis Loan II) and an apron with S.W. (for Sarah Walters) 1774 (Victoria and Albert Museum, 105–1962), a sampler said to be Danish 1758 (Victoria and Albert Museum, T.27–1940), and many other samplers in Stockholm and Copenhagen dated 1800–1820.

Dresden work was used on caps and lappets, shirt ruffles, fichus and aprons. Muslin aprons seem to have been worn especially at weddings: Margaret Rose of Kilravock wore one at her wedding in 1702 and Lady Grisell Baillie bought one for Grisie's wedding in 1710. White aprons, often lace-trimmed, were worn by children of both sexes in the seventeenth century, and probably the muslin aprons were home-made versions of the lace-trimmed variety. An even more obviously home-made muslin apron, which scarcely ranks as Dresden work, is in the Burrell Collection, Glasgow, and is said to have been worn at the christening of Prince Charles Edward Stuart in 1720 (Plate 58). Its provenance is unknown, but it is decorated with the arms of James VIII, the *Old Pretender*, with his cipher and the words "GOD BLESS AND RESTORE THE KING TO HIS OUNE". The apron may have been made by one of the exiled ladies of the Jacobite court. It is known that the banished Jacobites found it difficult to dress to their station on their inadequate means, with the revenues from their estates confiscated. Lady Nithsdale, whose straitened circumstances have already been mentioned (Chapter 10), wrote in March 1720 to her sister-in-law: "I wrote to my niece Mary Herbert, to see if she would be so generous as to give me some cloths, being realy in raggs, but as yet have had noe answer . . ." On the birth of Prince Charles Edward Stuart in 1720, she wrote: "Our Mistris was safely brought to bed of a son . . . upon the occasion of my Mistris's lying in, I have been forced to provide myself in cloaths that was a little decent. . . . I have the happiness to have had one handsome sute procured me by the means of a Cardinal who gott it from the Pope; but that is between you and I for I am forbid to let it be known. I have bought two others, the one as good as that, the other worse, for bad weather, being forc'd to walk to my Master's several times a day."[12] The muslin apron, with its ardent Jacobite sentiments, could well have been made for the same hopeful occasion.

In the second half of the eighteenth century, after the *tambour hook* had been imported from the Orient in about 1760,[13] chain stitch worked with the hook was employed, not only as an outline for Dresden work, but also to form sprays and trellis fillings. The hook, which took its French name from the round drum-like frame over which the material was stretched for working, could be used on silks and satins in coloured silks as well as on white muslin. Indeed, most of the chain-stitched satin waistcoats were worked in this way, and until the French Revolution, vast numbers were made in Paris workshops.

Tambouring became a fashionable pastime for ladies. Madame de Pompadour had a portrait of herself painted working with tambour hook at an oblong frame, not the conventional round one. The Ladies Waldegrave, the great-nieces of Horace Walpole, chose to be painted by Sir Joshua Reynolds seated round a work-table, with Lady Laura at the tambour, greatly to the disappointment of their great-uncle, who had hoped for a more classical pose. Tamboured muslin was soon being produced on a commercial scale.

The muslin on which the earlier Dresden work was embroidered was imported from India, but after the invention of Crompton's mule in 1779, British manufacturers were able to spin a very fine strong warp from cotton yarn. Mills, powered by water, were built to produce this yarn in Lancashire and Scotland, although at first it had to be hand-woven, a fine British muslin was produced, especially in the west of Scotland, which concentrated on this type of cloth. It was able to compete with and undersell the imported Indian muslin. This material was eminently suitable for decoration by the tambour hook, and a workroom was set up, in Edinburgh in 1782, by an Italian embroiderer, Luigi Ruffini. He had intended that his young apprentices, girls of six and seven, should be taught all kinds of needlework on the model of the continental workshops, and work on the designs drawn out by trained male designers, but the demand for flowered muslins was so great that he concentrated on supplying this, to the exclusion of other embroidery. The muslin manufacturers in the west of Scotland were quick to take up this way of decorating their muslin, and established workrooms of their own. By 1793, when the first statistical account of Scotland was published, parish ministers all over the west of Scotland reported the setting up of workrooms for tamboured muslin. The fashion for white muslin dresses stimulated the demand, and tamboured muslin was bought eagerly not only in Britain, but it even eluded Napoleon's Berlin decree of 1806, and was smuggled into the continent of Europe by the agents of Kirkman Finlay, the Glasgow cotton manufacturer.[14]

The tambour hook makes a continuous line of chain stitch. It was much used in India as a filling, but in Scotland at least, the chain stitch retained its lightness and grace in linear designs, sprays and trellises. Combined with the pulled stitches of Dresden work, it could still resemble lace (Plate 59), but because of the demand for dress materials, it became more a light and airy decoration for the muslin. When the war with Napoleon ended, the muslin, still as fine, but more firmly woven, became the basis for a different type of embroidered lace, this time with fillings of true needlepoint.

Professional designers were employed by the manufacturers of tamboured muslin and this later Ayrshire embroidery. Most of them were trained at the Drawing Academy set up in Edinburgh in 1760 by the Trustees for Fisheries and Manufactures to improve the standard of design especially in damask weaving. But the domestic needlewoman was not forgotten. *A Book of Designs suitable for the Tambour* was published in Edinburgh in 1779. *The Lady's Magazine* (1770–1832) showed borders and corners, though it is difficult now to find copies with the designs intact. A number of manuscript books compiled around the beginning of the nineteenth century show how the designs were collected and circulated by the domestic needlewoman.

EMBROIDERED LACE

Machine-made bobbin net, which imitated the net ground of lace made with bobbins on a pillow, began to be manufactured in increasing quantities after 1809 in the Nottingham area. It proved even more acceptable as a ground for home-made lace than did fine muslin. Delicate designs could be quickly darned into the meshes. In Ireland, it was used as the basis of two well-known lace industries, both founded as philanthropic projects: Limerick, started in 1829, in which the net is darned with different fillings; and Carrickmacross, introduced around 1830 in Co. Monaghan, where a fine cambric or muslin is applied to a net foundation.

Crochet, which took its name from the hook used in tambour embroidery, in which a chain stitch is made independently, without a woven foundation, but merely with a thread, appears to have evolved at the end of the eighteenth century, and became popular in Britain as a means of making lace in the first quarter of the nineteenth century.[15] Ursuline nuns introduced it to Ireland from France in the 1830's[16] and the characteristic raised rose and shamrock design of Irish crochet became enormously popular by the end of the century. Crochet is the only home-made lace to retain its popularity until the middle of the twentieth century. From the 1850's machine-made lace, manufactured in Nottingham and in St. Gallen, Switzerland, gradually won acceptance. The designs were copied from the well-known pillow and needlepoint laces. Only the discriminating few could buy, or indeed could recognize, 'real' (i.e. hand-made) lace, and only a few amateurs in Britain now keep the craft alive.

REFERENCES

1. Minutes of the Board of Trustees for Fisheries and Manufactures in Scotland, 1815.

2. *The Household Book of Lady Grisell Baillie 1692–1730*, p. 205.

3. *The Book of Caerlavrock*, privately printed Edinburgh, 1873, Letter 190, p. 185.

4. Op. cit., Letter 195, p. 191.

93

5. *The Household Books of Lord William Howard of Naworth*, [ed.,] George Ormsby, Surtees Society, Durham, Vol. LXVIII, 1834, pp. 189 and 258.

6. BATTISCOMBE, C. F., *The Relics of St. Cuthbert*, Oxford University Press, 1956, p. 111. I am indebted to the Dean and Chapter of Durham for permission to quote this description.

7. THOMSON, T. [ed.], *Collections of Inventories of the Royal Wardrobe and Jewelhouse*, Edinburgh, 1815, p. 233.

8. INNES, C., *The Black Book of Taymouth*, Bannatyne Club, Edinburgh, 1855, p. 350.

9. An unfinished piece showing the method of working is in the Musée d'Art Royaux, Brussels (No. 2562).

10. PALLISER, MRS. B., *A History of Lace*, Sampson Low, 1860, p. 375.

11. I am indebted to Miss Gertrude Townsend of the Museum of Fine Arts, Boston, for furnishing these biographical details of Rachel Leonard.

12. *The Book of Caerlavrock*, 1873, pp. 310 and 332.

13. ST. AUBIN, M. DE, *L'Art du Brodeur*, Academie des Sciences, Paris, 1770, p. 27.

14. I am indebted to Mrs. Monica Clough for this information from the archives of James Finlay and Son, Glasgow.

15. MISS LAMBERT, *The Hand-book of Needlework*, John Murray, London, 1842, p. 207.

16. BOYLE, E., *Irish Embroidery and Lacemaking 1600–1800*, *Ulster Folklife*, Vol. 14, 1966, p. 61.

12

Ayrshire Needlework

Embroidery on white muslin, now known as *Ayrshire needlework*, is an outstanding example of the interplay of foreign influences on a native embroidery. It began as a result of the American War of Independence, and ended because of the American Civil War. An Italian began the industry in 1782 when he introduced the methods of continental workrooms, using a hook that had been imported into France from India and China. The craft was carried to perfection by a Scotswoman who copied a technique she found on a French baby robe. The embroidery was worked on a material made to imitate and compete with Indian muslin, woven from very fine yarn brought first from India and then from the sea islands off Carolina, and finally from cotton grown on the mainland of America tended by African slaves. In spite of this cosmopolitan background, Ayrshire embroidery, or, to give it the contemporary trade name, *Sewed Muslin*, is a delicate, surprisingly durable and characteristic needlework, made in a whole range of different designs, between the years 1820 and 1870.

Worked in white cotton on a white cotton muslin, firmer than that used for tamboured muslin, it is characterized by the use of firmly padded satin stitch, stem stitch and beading, and is lightened by cut out spaces filled with many different patterns of needlepoint lace. It survives mostly on baby robes and caps, kept for sentimental reasons, but it was used also to embellish ladies' dresses and caps, men's shirt frills, women's riding habit shirts, pelerines (wide cape collars, fashionable 1830–1840), cuffs and collars, shawls and frills.

The manufacture of muslin began in Scotland as a result of the

American War of Independence, when the 'Tobacco Lords' of Glasgow, who had carried on there a very considerable trade with the colonies, found their supplies cut off and were forced to invest their capital elsewhere. They found an outlet in cotton, which, thanks to the inventions of such men as Arkwright and Crompton, could by that time be spun so finely and firmly that it began to compete with imported Indian muslin.

The Italian, Luigi Ruffini, first started a workroom in Edinburgh in 1782 and quickly evolved a professional method of embroidering Scottish muslin. He developed the use of a large rectangular frame with rollers at each end on which a whole length of uncut muslin could be stretched, and girls worked at either side, in place of the round drum-like *tambour* frame used by the domestic embroideress. White muslin gowns, once thought to have been a symbolic fashion of the French Revolution, but now believed to have originated in England, required yards of such muslin, plain or tamboured. British muslin was considerably cheaper than the Indian, which carried an import duty of anything from 18 per cent. in 1787 to 44 per cent. in 1813.

But by the end of the Napoleonic wars, fashion was already changing, and the simple white muslin gown began to lose its universal popularity. Lace, difficult to procure during the war, became fashionable again. In order to supply this need, an agent for the sewed muslin manufacturers in Ayr, Mrs. Jamieson, evolved a new type of decoration for the muslin, half lace, half embroidery, with fine needlepoint stitches filling the cut out spaces (Plate 60). She developed this technique from a French baby robe lent her by the widowed young Lady Mary Montgomerie, of Eglinton Castle, Ayrshire. Lady Mary had married her cousin, Archibald, Lord Montgomerie an *aide de camp* of the Duke of Wellington, and had accompanied her husband to Palermo in Sicily, where their son, Archibald, later 13th Earl of Eglinton, was born in 1812. Lord Montgomerie died in 1814, and the young widow brought back to Scotland a baby robe inset with lace stitches, worked by a Frenchwoman. This new technique inspired not only different designs, but a different method of working. The cumbersome frame was no longer required; instead, the material, with the design drawn on it,

Plate 53. Sampler signed and dated E G 1822, worked by Elizabeth Gardner. Darning patterns and needlepoint lace fillings with the centre medallion, with crown, date and initials, worked in Hollie point. Framed and divided by dark blue satin ribbon.

15·2 × 13·9 cm.

The Misses Muirhead

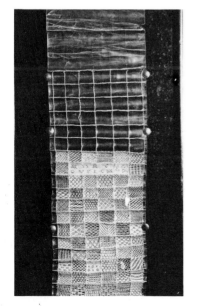

Plate 54. Sampler signed and dated Mary Quelch 1609. Needlepoint lace fillings worked on a foundation of laid thread on vellum. The name and date are worked in Hollie point (compare with the centre medallion of Elizabeth Gardner's sampler, Plate 53, also with the dated panels on Jenny Grant's sampler, Plate 55). This sampler of Mary Quelch appears to be the earliest dated white sampler so far recorded.

42·5 × 13·5 cm.

Dr. Douglas Goodhart

Plate 55. Sampler signed I.G. 1724 and Jenny Grant 1725. A note says 'daughter of Patrick Grant, Lord Elchies'. Patrick Grant had several daughters, but not one christened Jean. The eldest, Helen, was born in 1714. This seems a remarkably assured sampler to be worked at the age of 10. it is the earliest so far recorded of several very similar which seem to stem from a common source. White linen thread on linen. Geometrical satin stitch, cutwork, needlepoint lace filling and Hollie point. 23 x 21 cm. *National Museum of Scottish Antiquities.*

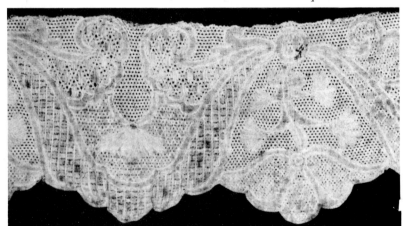

Plate 56. Shirt ruffle in Dresden work said to have been worn by Prince Charles Edward Stuart (Bonnie Prince Charlie) in 1745. This fragment, preserved as a Jacobite relic, shows a typically scrolled Dresden work design, the ground worked in a variety of drawn fabric stitches, the scrolls showing the plain material, this time apparently fine linen. Dresden work was made professionally on the continent of Europe, not only in Saxony, but in other parts of Germany and Scandinavia. It was taught in schools for young ladies, and was cheaper and more durable than fine pillow or needlepoint lace. Length of ruffle 90 cm. 6·7 cm. deep.

Fine linen thread on linen cambric.   no. 1928. 357.

The Royal Scottish Museum

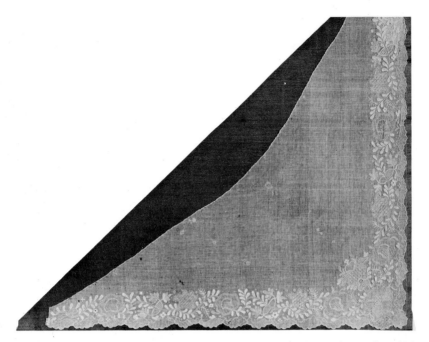

Plate 57. Kerchief signed and dated R L 1752. The initials are those of Rachel Leonard of Norton, Massachusetts, who was then 25 as she had previously worked a coat of arms with her name and age: Rachel Norton aged 13 1740. White linen thread on white muslin.
Buttonhole, chain and double back stitch (shadow work), and various drawn fabric stitches. no. 12.193. *The Museum of Fine Arts, Boston, Massachusetts*

Detail of Plate 57, showing the date, 1752 worked in eyelet holes in the centre of a flower. The initials, R L are worked in a similar manner at the other point of the kerchief, which is folded over in the plate.
The Museum of Fine Arts, Boston

Plate 58. Lady's Apron said to have been worn at the christening of Prince Charles Edward Stuart 1721. It is embroidered with the royal arms of Scotland, and the cypher I8 for James VIII ('the Old Pretender') and the mottos: GOD BLESS AND RESTORE THE KING TO HIS OUNE, and LET HIS ENEMIES NEVER HAVE POUER OVER HIM, and MAY THY ANGELS ALUAYS SUPPORT HIM.
White linen thread on white muslin.
Long and short stitch, buttonhole, eyelet holes and drawn fabric stitches. no. 199.
The Burrell Collection, Art Gallery and Museum, Glasgow

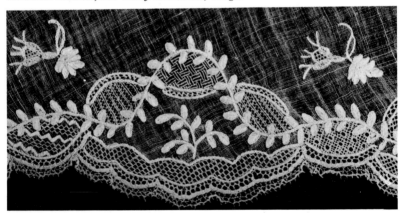

Plate 59. Detail of sleeve flounce ('engageante'), showing Dresden work filling outlined with tambour stitch, a chain stitch worked with a tambour hook. The flounce is edged with unheaded bobbin lace. 8·5 cm. deep.
Note the 'basket filling' (top) found also on the Swedish sampler 1678, Plate 52 and Elizabeth Gardner's sampler 1821, Plate 51.

Plate 60. Detail of the lower hem and flounce of a baby's robe, bought for a baby born 1863, showing typical Ayrshire needlework decoration: flower sprays in firmly padded satin stitch, with cut out spaces filled with needlepoint stitches. The delicate border with lace filled spaces is characteristic. White cotton thread on white cotton muslin.   11·4 × 17·5 cm.

Plate 61. Bodice and detail of skirt of baby robe in Ayrshire embroidery c..1850. These long robes, with triangular central panel with side flounce, triangular bodice and off the shoulder neckline, followed the style of women's dresses of 1830—1840. The cotton on which the embroidery is worked was 'British muslin', spun and woven in Scotland, and was given out to workers in their homes. The designs were drawn out by professional designers.
Mrs. E.M. Arthur

Plate 61a. Detail of skirt.

Plate 62. Crown of a baby's cap, 1863. The firm satin stitch outlines were first worked and the material cut away and filled with fine needlepoint lace stitches. The fillings are very similar to those found on the sampler of Mary Quelch 1609, Plate 54. Crowns could be bought separately and the caps made up at home if required. This was, of course, a day cap: a night cap was made of plain cambric.   Diameter 7·8 cm.

or stamped with wooden blocks in the case of repetitive designs for flounces and the like, was distributed to women who could embroider it in their own homes. In Irvine, they gathered together in each other's homes to share light and each other's company, while a child was paid a penny a week for keeping a supply of needles threaded for the workers. The embroidery was sent back to Glasgow to be made up, laundered, and boxed, and was sold not only in Britain, but on the Continent and in America. By 1857, it was estimated that some 80,000 women in Scotland, and 400,000 in Ireland were engaged in embroidering muslin in their own homes.[1]

The manufacturers employed professional designers. Ruffini sent his young male apprentices for a period of three years to the Trustees' Academy of Design, that produced so many Scottish artists, and the Glasgow manufacturers followed his example. In this way a nucleus of 'pattern drawers' was set up, who designed shawls and printed cottons, as well as linen damask and embroidery. Because it was intended for a competitive market, the standard of work was extremely high, as in continental workshops. Badly worked pieces, or those not finished on time, were rejected. A great many of the baby robes were made to individual orders, the finest muslin being the most expensive, and in several hundred examined, the writer has found only two of identical design. Both are unfinished, and are in the Kelvingrove Museum, Glasgow. The baby robes follow the style of women's dresses in 1830–1840, with high, often triangular bodices and a long decorated front panel, flanked by flounces that are often edged with an airy border decorated with lace stitches (Plate 61). The cap crowns, which could be bought separately to be made up at home (Plate 62), and the caps themselves (Plate 63) are exquisite examples of the lace maker's craft, entirely suited to their small scale. For some reason, no doubt in response to a demand, the caps are worked on linen cambric, not on Scottish muslin.

Like the Paisley shawl, which coincided roughly with Ayrshire embroidery, Ayrshire embroidery was an 'article of fancy', a style whose very popularity carried within it the threat of its own destruction. The end came suddenly with the American Civil War. Exports of cotton were prevented from leaving the Southern States. In 1861 Glasgow had imported 172,053 cwt. of cotton from America, but by 1864 this had fallen to 7,216 cwt.[2] The cotton industry in Lancashire was equally disrupted, and bitter hardship resulted. Although Lancashire gradually recovered after the war, Scottish manufacturers, who had specialized in muslins, did not, for the demand for plain and flowered muslins had diminished. The final blow to the embroidery industry was administered by the invention of a machine which could imitate embroidery. It was invented in 1828 by Josua Heilmann of Mulhouse and four machines made were sold in Lyons, Saxony, St. Gallen and Manchester. This last was sold to Henry Houldsworth who used it mostly for coloured embroideries on men's waistcoats.

Ironically, it was the St. Gallen machine that was the most successful, for it was adapted to imitate the white embroidery of Scottish sewed muslin. Even the designs and the circular 'wheel' fillings were reproduced, and much more cheaply than they could be achieved by hand, even at the depressed rates paid to the workers. This early white machine embroidery is often extremely good, with a characteristic rather flat satin stitch worked evenly in a twisted thread.

The sewed muslin industry had lasted some eighty years; it produced fine work of a standard and craftsmanship that could take its place in competition with the embroidery and lace from all other countries. This was the last occasion, since the Reformation, on which a professional embroidery industry on a large scale, was established in Britain.[3]

REFERENCES

1. STRANG, J., *The Embroidered Muslin Manufacture of Scotland and Ireland*, British Association for Science, Reports, 1857, p. 167.

2. BREMNER, D., *The Industries of Scotland*, Edinburgh, 1869, p. 288.

3. SWAIN, M. H., *The Flowerers*, W. & R. Chambers, Edinburgh, 1955, gives a fuller account of Ayrshire embroidery.

13

Berlin Woolwork

It used to be fashionable to dismiss all embroidery of the nineteenth century as tasteless and decadent, especially the so-called *Berlin woolwork*, mainly on the grounds that the patterns were unoriginal and the colours garish, because of the use of aniline dyes.

The Countess of Wilton, whose book, *The Art of Needlework* which was published in 1840, was the first historical account of needlework, describes the rise of Berlin woolwork:

About the year 1804–5, a print seller in Berlin, named Philipson, published the first coloured designs on checked paper for needlework. In 1810, Madame Wittich, who, being a very accomplished embroideress, perceived the great extension of which this branch of trade was capable, induced her husband, a book and print seller in Berlin, to engage in it with spirit. From that period the trade has gone on rapidly increasing. . . . By leading houses up to the commencement of the year 1840, there have been no less than fourteen thousand copper plate designs published. . . .

. . . Until 1831 the Berlin patterns were known to very few persons. . . . They had for some time been imported by Ackerman and some others, but in very small numbers indeed. In the year 1831, they, for the first time, fell under the notice of Mr. Wilks, Regent street (to whose kindness I am indebted for the valuable information on Berlin patterns given above) and he immediately purchased all the good designs he could procure, and also made large purchases both of patterns and working materials direct from Berlin, and thus laid the foundation of the trade in England. . . .[1]

The cross-stitch designs, worked in wool in vivid colours on canvas, sometimes with highlights in silk, or glass or metal beads, were used for chair seats, fire-screens, pictures, bell pulls, cushions, carpets, men's slippers and braces, ladies' bags or pin-cushions. The designs were printed on squared paper, each square representing a stitch, and at first were coloured by hand.[2]

There were two reasons for the enormous success of Berlin patterns in Europe and America. By counting out the stitches, it was possible for a painstaking needlewoman to obtain a far greater degree of realism and fidelity to the chosen design than had been possible when it was drawn out on canvas by an indifferent draughtsman. Secondly, the wools were softer and took a faster, more brilliant dye than the hard twisted worsteds hitherto available. The dyestuffs used were not at first aniline compounds. The first aniline dye, Perkin's *Mauvine*, was not introduced until 1856, and was followed by *Magenta* in 1860. Great improvements had been made in the science of dyeing, however, during the first half of the nineteenth century, and although the old vegetable dyestuffs, such as madder, indigo and logwood, were still used, new mordants and the *chemical dyes*, among them *Prussian blue* and *Manganese bronze*, were introduced, resulting in new colours which were not so fugitive as the earlier vegetable dyes. The vivid colours chosen for Berlin woolwork were not a new taste on the part of nineteenth-century needlewomen. The muted shades of worsted we see on canvas worked in the eighteenth century and earlier are not the colours chosen by the needlewomen themselves, but have faded. In unused pieces, like the uncut set belonging to Lord Crawford, or the slips at Traquair, the wools, which have not been exposed to light, are in startling, intense colours.

The wool supplied for working the new designs was dyed in Berlin and manufactured in Gotha. It was a soft wool from Saxony, where the flocks had been improved by the introduction of Merino sheep from Spain by the Elector in 1765. This wool, with its long silky staple, absorbed dye more readily and was very pleasant to work with, giving a smooth, even surface.

It is true that the designs, being printed, were not original; they were indeed frequently copies of paintings by Landseer and other artists, of animals, episodes from Sir Walter Scott's writings and the familiar Old Testament scenes of Esther, Jephthah's daughter and the Finding of Moses. But to any reader who has read so far, it will be evident that originality was never the primary aim of the domestic needlewoman, and that printed sources of one kind or another had been used as pattern designs for embroidery at least since the sixteenth century. Apart from the use of squared paper, which was a new development, Berlin designs merely followed the traditional pattern of the previous centuries. Geometrical designs for lace and darned net (lacis) had been printed in the earliest pattern books, and this had continued on the Continent, especially in Germany. Throughout the sixteenth and seventeenth centuries, embroidery pattern books continued to be produced, and in 1728 a book of cross-stitch designs was published in Augsburg by Martin Gottfried Crophius. These were mostly small motifs, however, more like those found on samplers, than the richly coloured pictorial patterns of Berlin woolwork.

The needlewoman's choice of designs remained remarkably constant. The little flowers painted on canvas for Mary Queen of Scots, the borage and carnation of the seventeenth century, the moss rose and auricula of the eighteenth century, each had its counterpart in the nineteenth century in the shape of the cabbage rose and passion flower of Berlin work. The birds, like the turkey which had recently been introduced from Mexico, had been engraved by Collaert, and printed by Thomas Johnson and Peter Stent to be worked by Stuart needlewomen; the Victorian embroideress had instead a bird taken from Audubon's *Birds of America*, published in 1827, which portrayed the brilliantly plumaged birds of north America. The beasts which Mary Queen of Scots chose from Conrad Gesner's *Historia Animalium* . . . published in 1551, now became the dogs and stags painted by Landseer, widely reproduced in engravings. The engravings of scenes from the *Aeneid* and *Georgics* of Virgil, known to every schoolboy, illustrated in Ogilby's handsome edition, and used by needlewomen of the eighteenth century, were replaced by the equally familiar scenes from the romantic narrative poems and novels of Sir Walter Scott. Even the royal portraits of the Kings and Queens published by Stent and used in the seventeenth century as models for Esther and Ahasuerus (or as Solomon and the Queen of Sheba), might be thought to find a counterpart in the portraits of the young Prince of Wales, attended by a large crouching dog.

Like the chair seat designs of the eighteenth century, Berlin patterns spread all over Europe, although the Countess of Wilton noted: "France consumes comparatively few Berlin patterns. The French ladies persevere in the practice of working on drawings previously traced on the canvas . . ." This practice has persisted till modern times in France. It has always been possible in Paris, as it was in the time of Catherine de Medici and her daughter-in-law, Mary Queen of Scots, to get an individual design drawn out on canvas or other material for working.

But in other countries, where so long a tradition of professional workshops with their trained draughtsmen was missing, needlework had become a domestic, mainly middle-class occupation, and in these countries: Germany, Britain, Holland, Scandinavia and North America, Berlin patterns and the bright new wools were greeted with enthusiasm. The counted squares enabled the chosen picture to be reproduced with a greater accuracy in drawing and shading than had ever before been possible. Indeed, the Berlin designs introduced into British needlework a Germanic meticulousness much admired by the needlewomen of the day, and considered greatly superior to the disproportionate figures and flowers of seventeenth-century canvas work. It is irrelevant to condemn the Victorian needlewoman for her preoccupation with fidelity to nature because it is no longer to our taste. The most admired needlewoman of the century, until her death in 1845 at the age of 90, was Miss Mary Linwood, who reproduced in faithful detail paintings by famous artists. The worsteds she used were specially dyed for her, and her needlework pictures, in long and short stitch, mirrored perfectly the tones and shading of the paintings they copied. "Perhaps," wrote the Countess of Wilton, "Miss Linwood will consider her greatest triumph to be in her copy of Carlo Dolci's *Salvator Mundi* for which she had been offered, and has refused, three thousand guineas." Miss Linwood is said to have bequeathed this panel to Queen Victoria.

Not every needlewoman could attain the heights of Miss Linwood's art, but thanks to the squared paper patterns of Berlin work, even the least skilled could reproduce in cross stitch the animal studies of Sir Edwin Landseer. Designs could be adapted to suit a special occasion. A group of ladies in Montreal worked a design of a small child in petticoats with a Newfoundland dog, and inscribed it: *The Young Bruce, First Lord of Canada* (Plate 64) in honour of the birth in Canada in 1840 of a son and heir to the Governor General, the Earl of Elgin and Kincardine. It was presented to the Governor General and still remains in the possession of the family. The picture was a favourite subject, and greatly resembles those showing the young Prince of Wales, who also is frequently depicted with a large dog.

Berlin designs and wools could be sent to those far away from shops. They were even sent to India, and many panels and fragments survive which were worked there by the Marchioness of Dalhousie (1817–1853), daughter of the 8th Marquess of Tweeddale. (Her husband was Governor General of India from 1848 to 1856.) The panels include the *Finding of Moses, Hagar and Ishmael, Jephtha's Daughter,* and *By the Waters of Babylon,* as well as studies by Landseer of the Scottish Gamekeeper and the English Gamekeeper, and other pictures and flower pieces. In spite of her frail health, she accompanied her husband on all his official journeys, even, it is said, to the Himalayas where no white woman had been before. Everywhere she went, her sewing accompanied her. She was an excellent horsewoman, but failing health obliged her to be carried in a litter and a drawing of her survives, carried by four servants, her hat shading her eyes, busily stitching, as she was borne along. In 1853 she became so ill that she was sent home in the hope that the long sea voyage would revive her, but she died before reaching England.

Four squares of a carpet also survive, together with a hearth rug to match, showing typical full-blown roses and the passion flower on a pale green ground worked in a delicate diaper pattern (Plate 65). The carpet was begun by her mother and sisters, and intended for the drawing-room at Dalhousie Castle. Her mother, it is said, worked the green ground. When the news of her death at sea reached them, the carpet was put away unfinished.

Stool tops and chair seats were also made in Berlin woolwork. Sometimes the worker prudently substituted the harder, more durable worsted for the soft Berlin *Zephyr* wools. But for fire-screens and glazed pictures they were delightful to use, covering the canvas evenly and comfortably, and providing a rich texture, especially when silk highlights were introduced.

Three-dimensional effects could be obtained in *Raised Berlin Work*, where a looped stitch, worked over a gauge, was used and then cut by scissors to give a sculptured velvet effect. Pictures of flowers, especially roses, and birds, survive in this technique. *The Englishwoman's Domestic Magazine* of June 1863 gives the pattern for a watch holder in the shape of a red rose, with a note that the work, when finished, could be sent to Mrs. Wilcockson, 44 Goodge Street, London, to be cut and finished professionally for the sum of 2*s*. 6*d*.

Criticism of Berlin patterns began as early as 1843.[3] In *Hints on Ornamental Needlework as applied to Ecclesiastical Purposes* by C.E.M., the author condemned the designs as unsuitable and too foreign for English churches. Church architects interested themselves in ecclesiastical embroidery, notably Pugin (1812–1852). They urged a close study of, and return to, ancient native designs. Societies, such as the *Ladies Ecclesiastical Embroidery Society* (1854), were established "to supply altar cloths of strictly ecclesiastical design either by reproducing ancient examples or by working under the supervision of a competent architect".

The study of ancient embroideries received a further impetus by the foundation, in 1872, of the Royal School of Art Needlework which found a home three years later in Exhibition Road, South Kensington. The South Kensington School, as it came to be called, under the active presidency of H.R.H. Princess Christian of Schleswig Holstein, was instituted with the two-fold aim of providing employment for poor gentlewomen and improving the standard of embroidery. The commissions undertaken were of a very high standard of craftsmanship, to the designs of William Morris, Walter Crane and other artists and architects. Another valuable service lay in the preparation of work for the domestic needlewoman, with lessons if she required them. The Royal School also undertook to repair and restore old embroideries.

Other schools with similar aims were set up in Britain in the 1880's. One which still survives is the Wemyss School of Needlework, founded in the 1880's by Miss Wemyss (Lady Henry Grosvenor) to give employment to miners' wives in the Coaltown of Wemyss. Its philanthropic help is no longer required, but the school continues to prepare work to individual orders and to repair old needlework.

The study of old needlework, with its faded colours, led to condemnation of the brilliant shades of Berlin woolwork, which had occupied domestic needlewomen so happily for half a century, and the 'aesthetic' movement towards the end of the century accelerated the demand for paler, subtler colours. Not all domestic needlewomen could afford to have designs drawn out to order by one of the Schools of Needlework, though their influence on taste and craftsmanship was far-reaching. Instead, there was a choice of printed designs in women's magazines, and publications by firms selling embroidery threads, such as Briggs of Manchester, or D.M.C. of Mulhouse, Alsace. Block printing of cotton muslin had been used by the Glasgow manufacturers for flounces and edgings in Ayrshire embroidery. It was now adapted to supplying such articles as chair backs and cushion covers to be sold in shops for working at home. A design could be drawn out on thin paper, and pricked through and pounced (powder rubbed through the prick holes) to trace a design on to the cloth. This 'pricking and pouncing' was the traditional method of transferring designs and dated from the Middle Ages. A new invention was the design printed in a bituminous ink or varnish, which could be transferred to the cloth by the pressure of a warm smoothing iron. These 'iron-on' transfers, invented by three employees of William Briggs, Manchester, in 1875, sold in vast numbers; they could be bought from shops or obtained by post from women's magazines. Like the Berlin patterns, they were a great boon to the needlewomen living in remote districts, but they too were finally condemned for their lack of originality, though even now they are still used to a limited extent.

Berlin woolwork did not die suddenly, in spite of the derision of the intellectuals. The designs and wool were used until the end of the century. Canvas work made an admirable covering for chairs, stools and *prie dieux*, and many people were undeterred by the criticism that it was in bad taste. This type of needlework continued to be used to furnish houses, to raise funds and to be given as presents to suitable recipients. A four-leaved screen survives, containing twelve glazed panels of Berlin woolwork, eight floral and four pictorial. These were worked by twelve young ladies in the Carse of Gowrie in 1860, and the completed screen was raffled in order to raise funds for the projected School for Ministers' Daughters (later Esdaile School, Edinburgh) (Plate 66). Embroidered slipper tops for men, worked in Berlin wools, made personal, though not apparently always acceptable gifts, judging from the number that were put away without being made up. Such a pair presented to the Duke of Wellington about 1850 is preserved at Apsley House, but these are worked in Florentine stitch, not the characteristic cross stitch. Others remain, with a Newfoundland dog, or a water lily and bulrushes worked on each toe. One pair from Perthshire has a lively pony's head on each toe, and is daringly inscribed in cross stitches of magenta wool: *To Mr. E. McRae from an admirer.* The recipient, alas, never wore them (Plate 67).

However amusing or unsuitable this choice of design may appear to us now, it is as characteristic of the epoch, and is no less irrational, than the open pea pod on the Elizabethan coif, or the rhinoceros on the Mellerstain panel. In many respects, the Victorian needlewoman is not given the credit she deserves. Due perhaps to the German influence of the court, the standard of execution among domestic needlewomen was far higher than it had been for many centuries. Meticulous stitchery was admired for its own sake. But it was also a period of great technological invention and curiosity about mechanical techniques. This curiosity is reflected in the desire of the domestic needlewoman to learn new methods of embroidery, new stitches, and to use new materials. Some, indeed, were old methods re-learnt: the study of old embroideries provided a rich source of new stitches. More comfortable travel encouraged more women to venture abroad and they brought back pieces from Italy, from

106

India and from the Aegean, which were studied and copied. Improved methods of indoor lighting, and a still plentiful supply of domestic servants, freed the Victorian middle-class housewife from many tasks that had occupied her ancestors, and gave her more leisure for needlework. Men's and even women's underclothes gradually ceased to be made at home, and embroidery took the place of plain sewing.

The urge to learn new methods of needlework was met by the publication, in books and women's magazines, from the 1860's onwards, of stitches and techniques of all kinds, not only for embroidery, but for crochet, knitting, hairpin lace, Teneriffe lace, macramé work, tatting, beadwork and other related crafts. This interest in technique, rather than design, satisfied the delight in variety that has always characterized needlewomen in these islands. Books dealing with technique were extremely popular: Caulfield and Saward's *Dictionary of Needlework* (1882) and the D.M.C. *Encyclopaedia of Needlework* by Thérèse de Dillmont, the English edition of which was first published in 1870 and is still in demand, were among the first of many such publications that have continued to the present day.

REFERENCES

1. THE COUNTESS OF WILTON, *The Art of Needlework*, London, 1840, pp. 397–9.

2. MORRIS, B., *Victorian Embroidery*, Herbert Jenkins, London, 1962, gives a detailed study of Berlin woolwork.

3. MORRIS, B., op. cit., p. 88.

14

The Amateur and the Artist

By the end of the nineteenth century, many embroiderers in Britain had begun to grow self-conscious about colour and design. Berlin woolwork, which had enjoyed wide popularity for more than half a century, had become old-fashioned, and did not accord with the 'aesthetic' style of furnishing, that had a strong Japanese flavour. Exhibitions of historic needlework, such as the Loan Exhibition of historic needlework 1873, at the South Kensington Museum, or that held in the Museum of Science and Art, Edinburgh, in 1877, evoked great interest in ancient embroideries. The Schools of Needlework renovated and remounted pieces, making them into screens, cushions and counterpanes. By the 1890's samplers and needlework pictures of the seventeenth century began to be collected. This study of ancient embroideries strengthened the mistaken belief that the faded colours were those actually used by the workers. These muted shades were adduced as evidence of the superiority of the old vegetable dyes and the better taste of needlewomen of past ages.

On the other hand, aniline dyes were condemned, not only for their strident tones, but for their fugitive qualities: a fault that was later to be rectified. "It would be pleasant," wrote May Morris in 1893 in an essay on *Colour*[1] "if in purchasing silk or cloth one had not to pause and consider 'Will it fade?' meaning not 'Will it fade in a hundred, or ten, or three years?', but 'Will it fade and be an unsightly rag this time next month?' I cannot see that Aniline has done more for us than this."

May Morris's father, William Morris, whose restless genius led him to master every craft in which he was interested, contributed an authoritative essay in the same volume on *The Art of Dyeing*, extolling the old dyestuffs, though admitting the impermanence of some of them: "Any one wanting to produce dyed textiles with any artistic quality in them must entirely forego the modern and commercial methods in favour of those which are at least as old as Pliny."

William Morris and the Arts and Crafts Society also had trenchant criticism of the current *needlepainting* in silk, and by implication, the designs of Berlin woolwork: "Modern design (of embroidery) is frequently naturalistic, and seems rather to seek after a life-like rendering of the object to be embroidered than the decoration of material."[2] Morris believed passionately that a designer for a craft should also be a craftsman, and it is characteristic of his energy that he should embroider a piece himself, and with his wife, unpick old work before making new designs of embroideries for others to work.

That the designer should also be a craftsman is not, perhaps, quite the same thing as saying that all craftsmen should make their own designs. Morris himself drew out many designs for embroideries for others to work. Some were executed in the workroom of his firm, founded in 1861; some were traced for sale to domestic embroiderers.

A new direction was given to teaching of embroidery in 1885, when Francis H. Newbery was appointed Principal of the Glasgow School of Art. Although primarily a painter, he, like Morris, believed in the equal importance of all the decorative arts. He had a profound influence on Charles Rennie Mackintosh, the architect, who was an evening student at the School of Art, as well as on Mackintosh's wife, Margaret Macdonald, who contributed embroideries to her husband's interiors. In 1894 a needlework and embroidery class was started by Jessie Newbery, wife of the Principal, who had herself been a student at the school. She was joined by Ann Macbeth (1875–1948) when they enlarged the classes to include the training of women teachers, and a new method of teaching needlework in schools was evolved. They discredited the old system of teaching young children to do fine stitchery, a method which had been followed since at least the sixteenth century, as we know from surviving samplers. Instead, Ann Macbeth laid emphasis on simple stitches, from which a design could be built up, line upon line, or used around an elementary shape, such as a circle or leaf, which could be drawn out by the worker herself on to the cloth. Traced designs were banned. This is the teaching still followed in schools in this country today.

In all art colleges, where embroidery is now a subject, originality of design is the primary aim, and with the bewildering array of new and synthetic materials and threads, most of the needlework produced is naturally tentative and experimental. Since students there are selected for their talent in drawing, and are being trained as artists or art teachers, designs are first sketched out on paper, and follow modern painting very closely. Fortunately, with its abstract shapes and preoccupation with texture, modern painting makes admirable patterns for textile designs, especially embroidery. These patterns can be carried out in various types of stitchery or appliqué, ranging from fabric collage attached with gum and the minimum of stitches, to the traditional gold work on linen applied to a rich background. The new materials have given much inspiration to the designers of liturgical garments and altar furnishings for Anglican and Roman Catholic churches. But the pre-eminent position held by painting as a subject in most art colleges, and the dependence upon it as a primary source of embroidery design, is demonstrated by the fact that the largest proportion of finished pieces are intended as wall panels. They are still, in fact, needlework pictures, often framed and glazed to emphasize the similarity.

This method produces artists who work in embroidery, but it does nothing to resolve the dilemma of the domestic needlewoman who, without talent or training in drawing, is urged to shun the designs of others and produce something original. Since the Reformation, women in Britain have found great delight in embroidery; the pleasure lies in the choice of colours, the mastery of intricate stitches, the making of something beautiful, which, like the creation of a garden, may survive one's own lifetime. In the past, a design may have been copied from an engraving, or bought ready sketched on the material, but today it is difficult to find a pleasing design ready traced, and it is often too expensive to commission an artist to make one.

THE AMATEUR AND THE ARTIST

Organizations such as the Women's Institutes, and the Embroiderers' Guild, attempt to help the amateur in the building up of design. The Embroiderers' Guild, established in 1906, originally admitted only needlewomen of high technical competence. Evidence of this had to be submitted before admission. This is no longer required, and the Guild, with branches in many parts of Britain and overseas, exists to help the amateur; by examples, classes and publications, to achieve a very high standard of technique and design. The Needlework Development Scheme, set up in Glasgow in the 1930's, had similar aims. A collection of embroideries, both ancient and modern, were on loan to schools and women's organizations in England and Scotland, and attractive and simple books of stitchery were published at low cost. Distinguished embroiderers were appointed Directors for a limited period, including, in 1948, Ulla Kockum, a Norwegian, who brought a strong Scandinavian influence into the country by her work and teaching. The Needlework Development Scheme terminated in 1960, but its influence still continues, especially in amateur work.

The tradition of centuries is difficult to shed, and in spite of the influence of abstract painting, natural objects such as flowers, birds and animals continue to serve as a source of inspiration to the amateur as well as the professional embroiderer. One of the few needlewomen to use stitchery alone as the basis of design was Mrs. Foster, who held an exhibition of her work, which she called *Wessex Stitchery*, in the Medici Galleries in London in March 1934, when she was then over ninety years of age. She had evolved interesting and deeply textured small panels. Some, embodying a verse or motto, were richly encrusted with variations of well-known stitches, usually worked in a linen thread, sometimes coloured, on a handwoven ground. But she appears to have founded no school, and her methods have not been continued.

Stitches worked by counting the thread, using an evenly woven linen, offer the worker without talent for drawing the best means of building up a design. This method was used with success by Mrs. Arthur Newall, who established the Fisherton de la Mere Industry in about 1890 which lasted until her death in 1922. This industry in Wiltshire gave employment to about 42 people, of all ages and

111

both sexes. She taught them first a simple stitch on linen in counted thread, and as they became proficient, showed them how to build up a design, though she drew out the more elaborate designs herself. She was exacting about finishes, and employed two good pillow lace makers, and one worker who specialized in tassels and edges. Other small industries were started to help the wounded in the First World War, and others unable to lead an active life. As at Fisherton de la Mere, stitches and patterns, taken mostly from old Italian linen embroideries, were taught to the workers.

There were many other historical techniques revived, and all were eagerly learned by the amateur needlewoman. The earliest published designs in the sixteenth century were for lacis, a darned linen embroidery on a foundation of knotted net. This was taught in Edinburgh by 'Carita' (Mrs. Isabel A. Simpson), who also published a textbook on the subject.[3] She insisted, however, on historical designs being preserved and followed, and discouraged originality. In the 1940's, the stitches of eighteenth-century Dresden work were revived, and greatly influenced by Scandinavian embroidery. Instead of the fine and exacting muslin, a smooth, loosely woven linen was used to make table mats and tray cloths. These stitches were taught in Scandinavia until well into the nineteenth century, as the number of surviving samplers testify (see Chapter 11).

But undeterred by the discussions about designs and originality, countless women throughout the present century, passionate needlewomen who were entranced by the problems of technique, but conscious of their limitations as artists, have continued to undertake ambitious embroideries for their homes and for posterity. Nina, Countess of Strathmore, who died in 1938 and was the mother of H.M. Queen Elizabeth the Queen Mother, embroidered bed furnishings for two four-poster beds at Glamis, one with the initials of all her ten children on the tester. There were many other notable needlewomen. Many of them have shared their knowledge and pleasure with others, in classes, and in the activities of the Women's Institutes, and other organizations. The Hon. Rachel Kay-Shuttleworth, who died in 1967, should be mentioned here. She was remarkable for her practical and encyclopaedic knowledge of lace

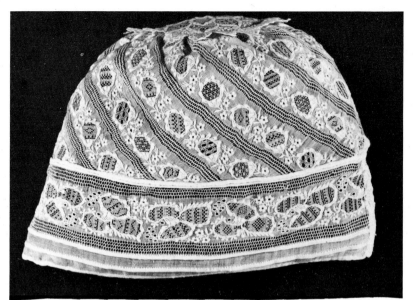

Plate 63. Cap belonging to the crown in Plate 62. Ayrshire needlework. Unlike the baby robes and other articles decorated with this embroidery, the baby caps, with very few exceptions, were made in linen cambric, not British muslin.

White cotton thread on white linen cambric.   11·4 cm. from crown to edge.

Collection of the late Mr. John Jacoby

Plate 64. Berlin woolwork picture inscribed THE YOUNG BRUCE, FIRST LORD OF CANADA, worked by ladies in Montreal and given to James, Earl of Elgin, Governor-General of Canada, 1846—1854, to commemorate the birth in Montreal of his eldest son, on 16th May 1849. Coloured wools on canvas. Cross stitch. 33·3 x 40·6 cm.
The Earl of Elgin and Kincardine.

Plate 65. Square for a carpet, one of five such squares, worked by the daughters of the eighth Marquess of Tweeddale, for their sister, who was married to the Marquess of Dalhousie, Governor General of India from 1848 to 1856. The carpet was intended for the drawing-room at Dalhousie Castle, but was never put together on account of Lady Dalhousie's early death in 1850 at the age of 33. The green ground was worked by their mother. A hearth rug to match also exists.

Silk and wool on canvas.

Cross stitch: Berlin woolwork. · 88·9 cm. square.

Lady Brown Lindsay

Plate 66. *The Pony Ride*. One of twelve panels incorporated into a heavy wooden screen. The panels were worked by twelve young ladies in the Carse of Gowrie, Perthshire, in 1860 and made into a screen which was raffled in order to raise funds to establish a school for the daughters of Church of Scotland ministers. The screen was subsequently presented to the school.
Berlin woolwork. Coloured wools on canvas.
Cross stitch.

The Governors of Esdaile School, Edinburgh

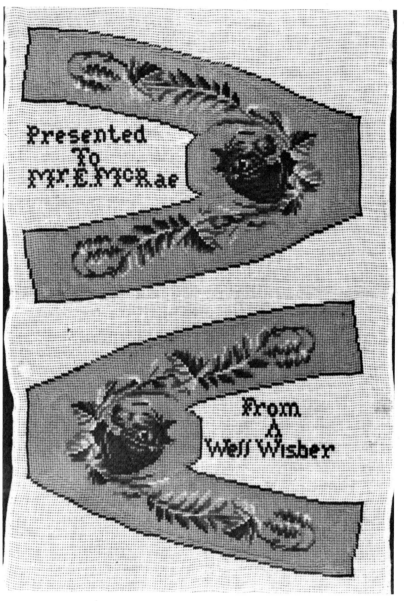

Plate 67. Man's slipper tops, unmounted. A pony's head on a dove-coloured ground, inscribed in magenta wool PRESENTED TO MR. E. McRAE FROM A WELL WISHER.
Berlin woolwork. Coloured wools on canvas.
Cross stitch.　56 × 39 cm.

Plate 68. Panel, the British Royal Arms, worked by Lady Evelyn Stuart Murray (1868—1940) the youngest daughter of the seventh Duke of Atholl. The arms are enclosed in a scrolled border, decorated with roses, thistles and shamrock, and the Prince of Wales's three feathers and motto ICH DIEN is at the base. Worked about 1912.

White cotton on fine cambric.

Satin stitch, stem stitch and drawn fabric fillings.   55·8 × 63·5 cm.

The Duke of Atholl

and most techniques in embroidery. She also continued, in an exceptionally busy life, to pass on her knowledge by teaching and writing. She amassed a large collection of textiles and books, now preserved at Gawthorpe Hall, Burnley.

Perhaps the most outstanding needlewoman of recent times was Lady Evelyn Stuart Murray (1863–1940), younger daughter of John, 7th Duke of Atholl. She was brought up at Blair Castle, with its rich collection of her ancestors' embroideries (see Chapter 9). She was shy and delicate, and took refuge in embroidery, making a highly personal and discriminating collection of foreign embroideries. She spent some time in Belgium, and her many samplers, preserved at Blair Castle, show a wide variety of exacting and almost forgotten techniques which she learned there. Her undoubted masterpiece, in the literal sense of that overworked word, is the superlative panel of white embroidery of incredible fineness, displaying the British Royal Arms (Plate 68), which she worked in about 1912.

Like so much of our embroidery in the past, it owes a great deal to the influence of the Low Countries and the techniques that she learned there. If all other embroidery of this century were to be destroyed, and this one piece, like St. Cuthbert's stole in Durham Cathedral, were to be the sole survivor of its age, it would offer mute, heraldic evidence of the excellence of British embroidery in the twentieth century.

REFERENCES

1. MORRIS, M., *Colour*. In *Arts and Crafts Essays by members of the Arts and Crafts Exhibition Society*, London, 1893, p. 382.

2. Op. cit., p. 356.

3. 'CARITA' (Mrs. I. A. Simpson), *Lacis*, Sampson Low and Marston, London, 1909.

Appendix

Letter from William Drummond to
Ben Jonson

To his Worthy Friend Master Benjamin Johnson.

SIR,

The uncertainty of your abode was a cause of my silence this time past; I have adventured this packet upon hopes that a man so famous cannot be in any place either of the City or Court where he shall not be found out. In my last I sent you a description of *Loch Lomond* with a map of *Inch-merinoch*, which may by your Book be made most famous; with the form of the Government of *Edinburgh*, and the Method of the Colleges of *Scotland*; for all inscriptions I have been curious to find out for you, the *Impressas* and Emblemes on a Bed of State wrought and embroidered all with gold and silk by the late Queen *Mary* mother to our sacred Soveraign, which will embellish greatly some pages of your Book, and is worthy your remembrance. The first is the Loadstone turning towards the pole, the word her Majesties name turned in an Anagram, *Maria Stuart, sa vertu m'attire,* which is not much inferiour to *Veritas armata.* This hath reference to a Crucifix, before which with all her Royal Ornaments she is humbled on her knees most lively, with the word *undique*; an *Impresa of Mary* of *Lorrain* her Mother, a *Phœnix* in flames, the word *en ma fin git mon commencement.* The *Impresa* of an Apple Tree growing in a Thorn, the word *Per vincula crescit.* The *Impresa* of *Henry* the second the *French King*, a *Crescant*, the word, *Donec totum impleat orbem.* The *Impresa* of King *Francis* the first, a *Salamander* crowned in the midst of Flames, the word, *Nutrisco et extinguo.* The *Impresa* of *Godfrey of Bullogne*, an Arrow passing throw three Birds, the word, *Dederitne viam Casusve Deusve.* That of *Mercurius* charming *Argos* with his hundred eyes, expressed by his *Caduceus*, two *Flutes*,

114

and a *Peacock*, the word, *Eloquium tot lumina clausit.* Two Women upon the Wheels of Fortune, the one holding a Lance, the other a *Cornucopia*; which *Impresa* seemeth to glance at Queen *Elizabeth* and her self, the word *Fortunæ Comites.* The *Impresa* of the Cardinal of *Lorrain* her Uncle, a *Pyramid* overgrown with *Ivy*, the vulgar word, *Te stante virebo*; a Ship with her Mast broken and fallen in the Sea, the word, *Nunquam nisi rectam.* This is for her self and her Son, a Big *Lyon* and a young Whelp beside her, word, *unum quidem, sed Leonem.* An emblem of a *Lyon* taken in a Net, and Hares wantonly passing over him, the word, *Et lepores devicto insultant Leoni Cammomel* in a garden, the word, *Fructus calcata dat amplos.* A Palm Tree, the word, *Ponderibus virtus innata resistit.* A Bird in a *Cage*, and a *Hawk* flying above, with the word *il mal me preme et me spaventa Peggio.* A Triangle with a Sun in the middle of a Circle, the word *Trino non convenit orbis.* A Porcupine amongst Sea Rocks, the word, *ne volutetur.* The *Impresa of* King *Henry* VIII, a *Portculles*, the word, *altera securitas.* The *Impresa* of the Duke of *Savoy*, the annunciation of the *Virgin Mary*, the word *Fortitudo ejus* Rhodum *tenuit.* He had kept the Isle of *Rhodes.* Flourishes of Arms, as Helms, Launces, Corslets, Pikes, Muskets, Canons and the word, *Dabit Deus his quoque finem.* A Tree planted in a Church-yard environed with dead mens bones, the word, *Pietas revocabit ab orco.* Eclipses of the Sun and the Moon, the word, *Ipsa sibi lumen quod invidet aufert*; glauncing, as may appear, at Queen *Elizabeth. Brennus* Ballances, a sword cast in to weigh Gold, the word, *Quid nisi victis dolor?* A Vine tree watred with Wine, which instead to make it spring and grow, maketh it fade, the word, *Mea sic mihi prosunt.* A wheel rolled from a Mountain in the Sea, *Piena di dolor voda de Speranza.* Which appeareth to be her own, and it should be *Precipitio senza speranza.* A heap of Wings and Feathers dispersed; the word, *Magnatum Vicinitas.* A Trophie upon a Tree, with Mytres, Crowns, Hats, Masks, Swords, Books, and a Woman with a Vail about her eyes or muffled, pointing to some about her, with this word, *Vt casus dederit.* Three Crowns, two opposite, and another above in the Sky, the word *Aliamque moratur.* The Sun in an Ecclipse, the word, *Medio occidet Die.*

I omit the Arms of *Scotland, England,* and *France* severally by themselves, and all quartered in many places of this Bed. The workmanship is curiously done, and above all value, and truely it may be of this Piece said *Materiam superabat opus*.

I have sent you (as you desired) the Oath which the old valiant Knights of *Scotland* gave, when they received the Order of Knighthood, which was done with great solemnity and magnificence.

W. Drummond.

July 1, 1619.

From: *William Drummond of Hawthornden. Works* 1711.

Glossary

Certain difficulties arise in attempting to describe the stitches found on old embroideries. Short of unpicking them, we are not always sure of how they were worked, nor do we always know what they are called by the needlewomen who worked them. Although a few are familiar, most of the stitches listed by John Taylor, the Water Poet, in the introduction to *The Needle's Excellency* (10th edition 1634) can only be guessed at:

For *Tent-worke, Raisd-worke, Laid-worke, Frost-worke, Net-worke*
Most curious *Purles*, or rare *Italian Cutworke*,
Fine *Ferne-stitch, Finny-stitch, New stitch* and *Chain-stitch*,
Braue *Bred-stitch, Fisher-stitch, Irish-stitch*, and *Queene-stitch*
The smarting *Whip-stitch, Back-stitch*, & *the Crosse-stitch*
All these are good and these we must allow
And these are everywhere in practise now.

Surprisingly, satin stitch, that most common of modern stitches, is omitted from this list, though it occurs in the longer list compiled by Randall Holme in his encyclopaedic book *The Academy of Armoury* published in 1688, and quoted by J. L. Nevinson in his *Catalogue of English Domestic Embroidery* (p. XX).

Many of the names by which we identify stitches are comparatively modern, given to them in the past eighty or ninety years. The stitch that we now call Roumanian, for instance, is very similar to that used to depict the vivid scenes on the embroidered strip cartoon that we now refer to as the Bayeux tapestry which was made while Roumania was still a part of the Byzantine empire. Roumanian stitch is not listed by Caulfield and Saward in their *Dictionary of Needlework* 1882. Similarly it is improbable that Holbein stitch was so called when it was employed with such assurance to

117

portray the figure of Christ and the Instruments of the Passion alike on both sides of the Fetternear Banner, as it was worked around 1521, when Hans Holbein the elder and his son Hans the younger were still both alive. Holbein stitch is illustrated by Caulfield and Saward, but its alternative, modern name—double running—appears to have been given after 1882.

Florentine or Hungarian stitch, worked in gradations of colour, is found on many seventeenth- and eighteenth-century samplers but is not listed in Caulfield and Saward. Worked in one shade, over a long and short count of thread, it was used as an interesting background on eighteenth-centu.y chair covers and fire-screens. The only stitch that corresponds with it is Irish stitch, illustrated in *The Handbook of Needlework* by Miss Lambert (1842), and also in Caulfield and Saward. This is a much simpler version than the often complicated count of the eighteenth-century patterns, but it seems very probable that the stitch we now call Florentine was the Irish stitch referred to by John Taylor and Randall Holme. Miss Lambert, however, mentions also a stitch called Hungary stitch among *Various Fancy stitches*: ". . . modifications of the five stitches already mentioned (Tent, Cross, Irish, Gobelin and German stitch) and it will be only necessary for us to name the principal recognized old English stitches; to attempt a description of them, would be alike tedious and useless. They are, ferne stitch, feather stitch, basket stitch, mat stitch, bead stitch, braid stitch, plait stitch, diamond stitch, square stitch, star stitch, wove Irish stitch, reverse cross stitch, mosaic flat stitch, brick stitch, Venetian stitch, Peruvian stitch, Hungary stitch, plaid stitch; but this must suffice. Innumerable are the stitches which are to be met with on the samplers worked for sale, both in England and Germany, and numberless the names applied to them, and it is easy to invent new stitches, as it is to invent new names for them" (p. 154).

For the sake of clarity, modern names have been given to the stitches found on the pieces described in this book, and the diagrams illustrate how they were worked. It should be borne in mind, however, that a needlewoman in the past did not always follow the orthodox method of working a stitch: she often adapted it to suit her own convenience. Long-armed cross stitch, for instance, is now usually worked horizontally from left to right, especially when the material is held in the hand. An embroideress seated at a long narrow panel in a frame, with a good deal of ground to cover, as in

118

the Hardwick panel, mentioned in Chapter 4 p. 25, naturally found it more convenient and comfortable to work the stitch vertically so that she did not have to stretch her arm or move her seat in order to complete a line. Since the days of Berlin woolwork, we have been taught that the upper stitch of cross stitch ought always to slant in the same direction: earlier needlewomen were not bound by this convention, and changed the direction at will, which often produced interesting textures.

Readers who wish to learn the acceptable modern way of working these stitches are referred to Mrs. Archibald Christie's *Samplers and Stitches* (1920) and Mary Thomas's *Dictionary of Stitches* (1934).

BLACKWORK

Fine black silk embroidery on white linen, sometimes enriched with metal thread and spangles. Intricate geometrical designs worked in double running are depicted on the linen worn in portraits by Holbein the elder (1465–1524) and Holbein the younger (1497–1543) (see Double running). In scrolled designs on surviving pieces the leaves and other spaces are often filled with minute diaper designs in great variety, or with fine speckling graduated to suggest modelling. See Nevison J. L. *Catalogue of English Domestic Embroidery*, 1938 p. 17.

CHAIN STITCH Fig. 1

A looped stitch found on some of the most ancient embroideries to have survived: those found at Pazyryk, northern Mongolia, and now preserved in the Hermitage Museum, Leningrad, dated to the fifth century B.C. Although it is common in Oriental embroideries, it is rarely found on pieces made in this country that can be dated before the Reformation. (See Tambour stitch.)

COUCHING

The method by which cord or thread is applied to the surface of materials and held down by small fine stitches.

CREWEL WORK

A term first used about 1860 for embroidery in coloured worsteds, or crewels (from *crewle* or *crule*, a thin worsted

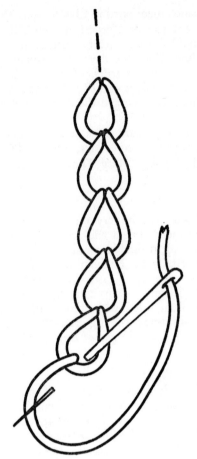

Fig. 1 Chain stitch

yarn), "Take silk or crewel, gold or silver thread, and make these fast at the bent of a hook." (Izaak Walton *The Compleat Angler*.) Crewel work is a more accurate term than Jacobean work to describe coloured wool embroidery upon twill, using a diversity of stitches, since this type of embroidery cannot be limited to the reigns of either James I or James II. (See Worsted.)

CROSS STITCH Gros Point. Fig. 2

An ancient stitch found (as an upright cross) in textiles from
Coptic burial grounds of the early Christian era, but rare on
medieval pieces in this country. It occurs, however, on the Syon
cope and a burse of the same period. In working, each stitch

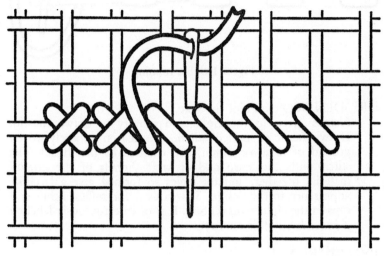

Fig. 2 Cross stitch

can be completed before proceeding to the next, or it can be
worked in two journeys as in the diagram. Ideally the top
stitch should always cross in the same direction, but in the
past the needlewoman did not always obey this rule.

DOUBLE RUNNING Holbein. Fig. 3

Caulfield and Saward give the alternative name Italian stitch.
It is usually worked in black silk on white linen, in geometric
lines often of great intricacy. It occurs on a fragment from a
burial ground in Egypt of the late medieval period, and is depicted by Holbein the elder in his paintings of SS. Elizabeth
and Barbara (Alte Pinakothek, Munich) and by Holbein the
younger in his portrait of Jane Seymour (Kunst Historisches

Museum, Vienna). It is eminently suitable for ruffs and cuffs as it is completely reversible.

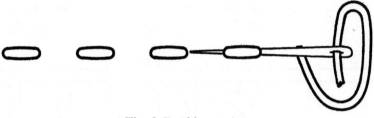

Fig. 3 Double running

DRESDEN WORK Point de Saxe.
Names given in the eighteenth century to drawn muslin. Drawn fabric or 'pulled' stitches worked on a loosely woven ground of linen or cotton, and counted by the thread. The stitch pulls the warp and/or weft threads of the ground material together, and the holes so formed give a lace-like appearance to the design. It was used for ruffles, fichus and caps in the eighteenth century. It is often erroneously labelled *Tønder lace* in this country.

EYELET HOLE Fig. 4
"The small opening in any material" (Caulfield and Saward). When worked on linen it is usually, but not always, made by 16 or 8 satin stitches all taken into a central hole, which is enlarged by the tension of the stitches. "Pie steek" in Scotland (John Galt).

FLORENTINE STITCH Hungarian, Bargello, Flame stitch. Fig. 5
All these are modern names for a straight stitch on canvas worked in zigzag lines, often in gradations of colour. Some modern writers distinguish between Florentine and Hungarian stitch according to the number of threads over which the line rises or falls, but the stitch is essentially the same and capable of many variations of line. Florentine stitches are found on seventeenth- and eighteenth-century samplers, but neither Miss Lambert (1842) nor Caulfield and Saward (1882) list any of these names. A simple version of Florentine is illustrated in

both books as *Irish stitch.* It may be, therefore, that Irish stitch, mentioned by both Randall Holme and John Taylor in

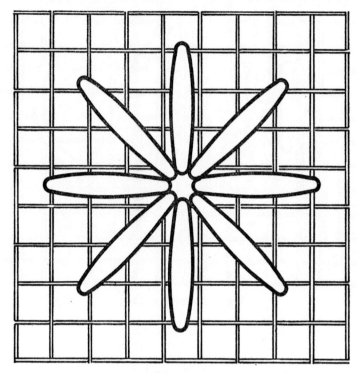

Fig. 4 Eyelet hole

the seventeenth century, is the old name for the modern Florentine stitch.

FRENCH KNOTS Fig. 6
The thread is wound round the needle and secured to make a knot, which lies on the surface of the material. The stitch is found on ancient Chinese embroideries. "The centres of many full-blown flowers, such as roses and dahlias, are sometimes represented by what is termed French knotting"—Miss Lambert.

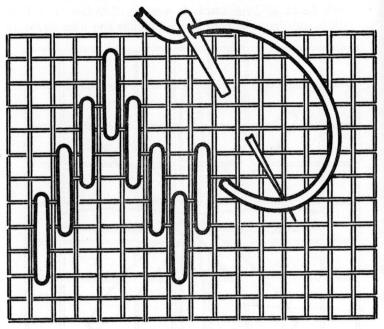

Fig. 5 Florentine stitch

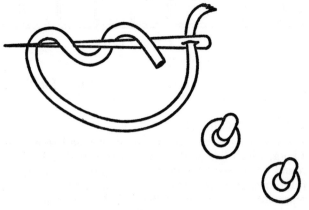

Fig. 6 French knots

GOBELIN STITCH Fig. 7

A straight canvas stitch over two warp threads resembling the horizontal lines of a Gobelin tapestry woven on a high warp loom. Miss Lambert (1842) gives a version (followed by

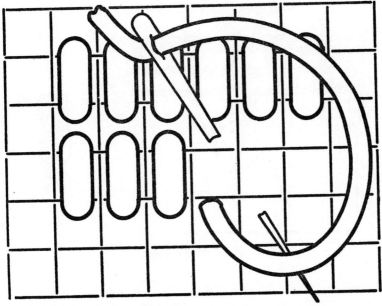

Fig. 7 Gobelin stitch

modern writers) over two warp and one weft thread which gives a firmer texture.

HOLLIE POINT Fig. 8

A knotted lace stitch detached from the material, worked in rows from left to right. A hole is left in the row each time a stitch is omitted, and these spaces form the basis of the design.

LACE STITCHES Needlepoint.

Looped or knotted stitches (see Hollie point) worked with a needle and thread, as distinct from lace made on a pillow with the thread wound on bobbins. Many lace stitches are variations of looped or buttonhole stitch, the arrangement of the holes giving each a different pattern.

In America the term needlepoint is now used for canvas work embroidery.

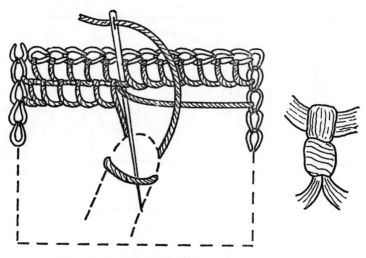

Fig. 8 Hollie point

LONG-ARMED CROSS STITCH. Long-legged cross stitch. Fig. 9
  A modern name for a stitch found on medieval embroideries and on a panel at Hardwick, with a design of oak leaves on a red ground. The stitch can be worked horizontally or vertically.

LONG AND SHORT STITCH Fig. 10
  A variation of satin stitch, in which the first line is given an even outline but the lower end of each stitch is alternately long and short. Stitches of equal length follow the spaces left in the first line. It was used in the seventeenth and eighteenth centuries where large spaces had to be covered or shading was required. A modern name.

NETTING Filet.
  A groundwork for lace, knotted over a gauge or mesh, in the same way as fishermen's nets are made. The square spaces in

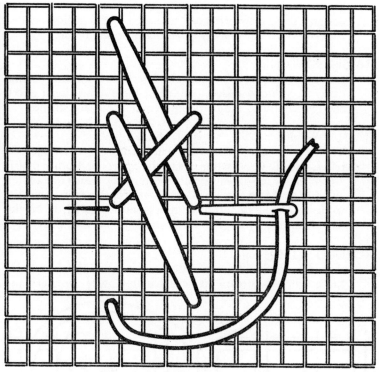

Fig. 9 Long Armed cross stitch

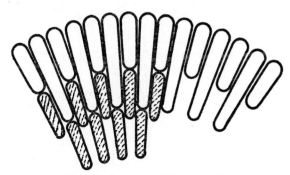

Fig. 10 Long and Short stitch

the net were often darned to make geometrical or pictorial designs, some of which were published in the earliest printed pattern books. Such lace is called *Lacis* or *filet* brodé.

RAISED STITCHES

Stitches which are knotted or detached from the ground material, giving a raised, padded or three-dimensional effect. See French knots, Hollie point, Needlepoint lace stitches.

RAISED WORK

The name given in the seventeenth century to embroidery in relief, usually upon satin, where the figures and other motifs are given a three-dimensional appearance by means of padding and detached lace stitches. *Stump work* for this type of needlework is "a modern and meaningless misnomer". J. L. Nevinson, *Catalogue of English Domestic Embroideries*, p. XXI.

ROCOCO STITCH Fig. 11

A modern name (the word *rococo* is not recorded before 1836) for a stitch occurring in seventeenth-century samplers and

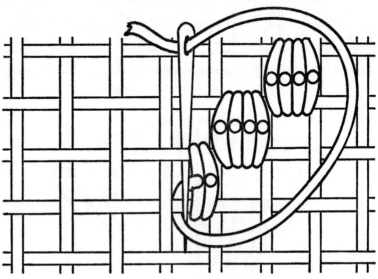

Fig. 11 Rococo stitch

panels, and in pieces after that date. It is a tied stitch, very similar to Roumanian, but worked in bundles, usually four or five stitches into the same hole. The bundles are worked diagonally on canvas or evenly woven linen. A fine stitch, usually worked in silk.

ROUMANIAN STITCH Fig. 12

A modern name for a tied stitch very similar to that used on the Bayeux tapestry. It can be worked closely together or spaced apart.

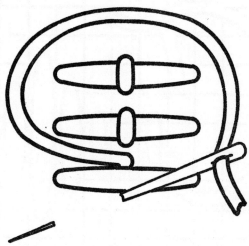

Fig. 12 Roumanian stitch

SATIN STITCH Fig. 13

A flat straight stitch, giving a smooth appearance when worked closely together, on firmly woven material. When worked by counting the threads, it is usually called *Geometrical satin stitch*. Satin stitch is listed by Randall Holme in the *Academy of Armoury*, 1688.

SLIPS

Literally, the slips or cuttings used for the vegetative propagation of plants, illustrated in Herbals and other books of

129

K

engravings in the sixteenth and seventeenth centuries. They served as needlework designs, and with birds and animals, also found in engravings, were embroidered in fine tent stitch on canvas, and then cut out and applied to cloth. "Ane rid skarlett tablecloth, shewed with bouk (carcasses of animals) and slips." Inventory of Tyninghame, June 1635. Fraser W., *Memorials of the Earls of Haddington* Ed. 1889, Vol. II, p. 300, no. 414.

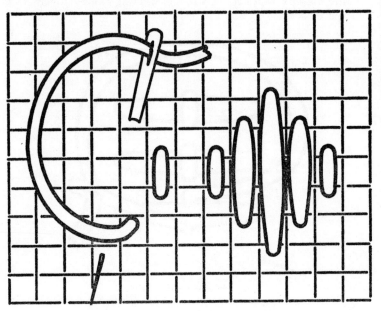

Fig. 13 Geometrical Satin stitch

SPLIT STITCH Fig. 14

Stem stitch in which the needle splits the thread which emerges from the previous stitch. The stitch is found on ancient embroideries from northern Mongolia now preserved in the Hermitage Museum, Leningrad, and on fragments found at Palmyra of the first century A.D. It was used extensively for faces and other fine details in the medieval *Opus Anglicanum*. A modern name, not listed by Caulfield and Saward, 1882.

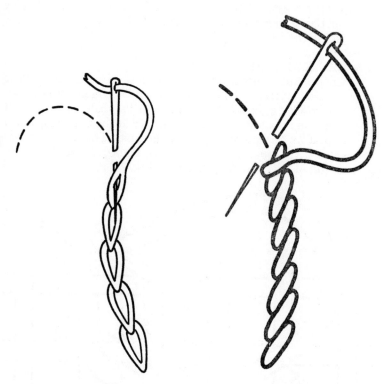

Fig. 14 Split stitch   Fig. 15 Stem stitch

STEM STITCH Fig. 15

Not listed by Miss Lambert, it is illustrated as *crewel stitch* by Caulfield and Saward. A line stitch. The line may be made thick or thin according to the angle of the needle. The thread should lie to the right of the needle; if thrown to the left, it is now named *outline stitch*.

STRAPWORK

A modern name first recorded 1854, for a flat tape-like Renaissance ornament. "*Strapwork*: A peculiar kind of ornament adopted extensively in the fifteenth and sixteenth centuries (particularly in Flanders and Germany) . . . which consists of

131

a narrow fillet or band, folded and crossed, and occasionally interlaced with another." Fairholt, *Dictionary of Terms of Art*, 1854. O.E.D.

TAMBOUR STITCH

Chain stitch worked with a hook instead of a needle. The material is stretched on a round drum-like frame, or *tambour*. The working thread is held beneath the material in the left hand, and hooked up on to the surface in short stitches, which appear as chain stitch, by the right hand. The technique was introduced from the Orient into France about 1760. St. Aubin M de, *L'Art du Brodeur*, Paris 1770, p. 27.

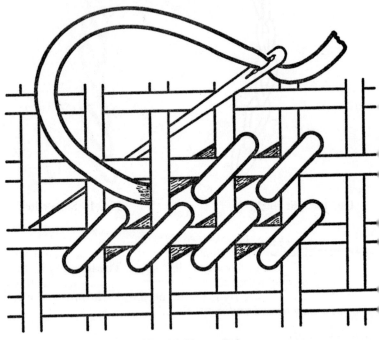

Fig. 16 Tent stitch

TENT STITCH Fig. 16

A half cross stitch across a warp and weft thread. From *tent*, the tenter or frame used by embroiderers to keep the canvas stretched and rigid while working the design. The stitch can be worked in a horizontal or diagonal line. The name *petit point* is used in Britain to describe tent stitch worked on fine mesh canvas or linen.

TIED STITCH
A long stitch which is tied down by a shorter stitch, as in Roumanian stitch.

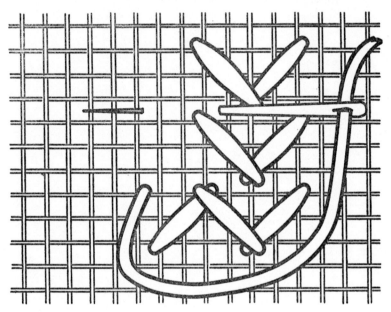

Fig. 17 Stitch in the Aninston panel and Burrell Valance

TURKEY WORK
A short woven pile, knotted on the loom in the same way as an oriental carpet, and not needlework at all; but it is generally listed with needlework, as it served to cover chairs and stools in the seventeenth century. ". . . Chaires and stools of Turky work, Russia or Calves Leather, cloth or stuffe, or of

needlework," Randall Holme, *The Academy of Armoury* Bk. III, Ch. XIV, p. 15.

STITCH ON THE ARNISTON PANEL AND BURRELL VALANCE (Plates 10 and 11) Fig. 17

This appears to be what is now called *Plaited Gobelin stitch* worked vertically instead of horizontally.

Index

135

INDEX

INDEX

137

INDEX

INDEX

INDEX